HOME-BASED

how to start a home-based

Pet-Sitting and Dog-Walking Business

Cathy Vaughan

Guilford, Connecticut

Text designed by Sheryl P. Kober

Library of Congress Cataloging-in-Publication Data

Vaughan, Cathy.
  How to start a home-based pet-sitting and dog-walking business / Cathy
Vaughan.
    p. cm.
  ISBN 978-0-7627-6083-1
  1. Pet sitting—Vocational guidance. 2. Dog-walking—Vocational
guidance. 3. Pets—Services for. I. Title.
  SF414.34.V38 2011
  636.088′7—dc22

                        2010040898

Printed in the United States of America
10 9 8 7 6 5 4 3 2 1

This book is dedicated to my dad, Skip Fereday, who instilled in me from a young age the love of all God's creatures. It was often said of him that kids and animals were drawn to him. From my first pet, "Mini" the poodle, to our first rescued stray dog, Lucky, the twenty-two hamsters we had at one time, numerous cats, and many other furry creatures you allowed to be a part of our family, you brought me to the devotion I have to animal care today. Without my dad's love and support, encouragement, and devotion over the years, my career as a pet care professional might not have seen fruition. For all you've done for me, I thank you dad and dedicate this book to you in loving memory.

Acknowledgments

This book would not have been possible without the support, help, and love of the many people in my life who supported me in my research and gave me encouragement to forge ahead.

I often comment to my clients that I am a much better pet sitter than I am accountant and records keeper. I heard those words run through my brain on numerous occasions during the writing of this book. As a pet sitter and animal lover, I knew the tools I wanted to share with the tidbits and insight, but getting them down on paper was the hard part. Thank you to the many people in my life who made this project possible.

This was truly a labor of love and was made possible primarily through the support of my incredibly wonderful and supportive best friend and husband, Phillip Vaughan. On any given day, he's found to be doing the laundry, helping our kids with their homework, or cleaning the kitchen. It's this day-to-day support in keeping our family going that has made it possible to grow our pet-sitting business into the family legacy it is today. During the many months that it took me to complete this project, he was virtually a single parent many of those days, making it possible for me to devote hour upon hour to my writing at the local library. Without his support, our business and thus this book would not have been possible.

Thank you to the many staff members at Pet Sitters International who've provided innumerable nuggets of wisdom over the course of the years of my membership, many of which you will find in this book. Thank you to those PSI staff members who sent me the information needed to complete areas of research into our industry, the behind the scenes information that made my writing complete. The pet-sitting industry is made up of some of the best people in the world, with the cream of the crop at the PSI office. Thank you for supporting me in my efforts to write this book and for your daily support of all of your members.

Thank you to Stacie Jaeger, my awesome office assistant, right hand gal and fabulous friend and to the staff of Cathy's Critter Care who saw to it that our standards of care were met even when I was absent from the front lines while writing. Having a team of pet sitters to bounce ideas off of and provide the information in this book was invaluable.

Finally, thank you to my mom, Carol and my three great kids, Collin, Ryan and Ainsleigh who were never ending in their understanding of the necessary absence needed to write this book. Thank you for allowing me the freedom to do the things that make my life complete.

Contents

Introduction

Pets are becoming true members of the family, being treated as such. Thus, pet owners are seeking reliable care for their pets and looking for a professional pet sitter to come to their home. People who work long hours and feel guilty about being away from their fur children are hiring dog walkers for mid-day care. Families are traveling for vacation and require the care of a professional pet sitter. Business people are being asked to leave behind their beloved pets more as they are asked to travel for work. The pet industry continues to thrive even in slowing economies and proves that pets are an integral part of our lives.

There is a definite need for the professional pet sitter. In the past people relied on the neighbor or kid down the street, but as pets have become a more important aspect of our family and as the security of homes has become an issue, people are turning to professionals to provide the much-needed care for their pets.

The professional pet-sitting industry is a new one, becoming a recognized profession only within the last twenty years. This book will guide you through the initial phase of imagining what your pet-sitting business will entail to the nuts and bolts of the daily work of being pet sitter, accountant, sales force, and complaint department. This can be intimidating when you start. In the words of Dave Ramsey, "you have to leave the cave, kill something, and drag it home" to make a living. Although there might be clients out there for your business, it will be your job to draw them to you and to ensure that the quality care you provide is the best they can find. One of the most enticing things about starting a pet-sitting business is that you can do it while you are still working in another job. So it doesn't have to be sink-or-swim. You can dog paddle along until the waters are smooth enough to break away.

Another great aspect of starting your own home-based pet-sitting business is that it can be done with little investment. There's no expensive equipment to buy or large inventories to keep on hand. People are paying you for your time with their pet and your expertise in dealing with animals.

Although in a sense you will be working alone, you will get to meet some of the best pet owners in the world. Some of these people will likely become good friends. As a professional pet sitter you will get to see mostly the good side of pet ownership. Unlike shelter workers, who provide an invaluable service, you won't have to deal with mistreatment of animals very often. Unlike veterinarians who have to deal with illness and death regularly, you get to focus your attention on the liveliness of your clients and to make their day more fun.

This book doesn't cover every aspect you will encounter as a pet sitter. Like I tell my staff, "I could tell you a thousand and one things about this business, and you'd encounter number one thousand and two." The pet-sitting profession is still new enough to be evolving. Don't be afraid to make your business your own and incorporate ideas from several sources. Working as a pet sitter requires good, old fashioned OJT (on-the-job training). As you move through your first year in business, you will undoubtedly establish your own way of doing things that suits your business and your market of pet owners. You will become more comfortable dealing with varying types of people and pets, scheduling challenges, and even learn from some bumps in the road. Pet sitting is a profession that definitely isn't the same every day and provides rewards that go way beyond the monetary income.

This book is not meant as a guide to the *only* way to start and run a pet-sitting business. Nor is this book meant as an endorsement as the only right way to run your business. It, however, will get you headed in the right direction with the sound and solid practices that have worked for many pet-sitting businesses that are maintaining their success for the long run. Some of these pet-sitting businesses are owned and operated by one indvidual after many years in business, and some have grown into huge companies that employ and contract out work to over fifty staff pet sitters. Where you take your pet-sitting business is up to you and your goals, but the work, clients, and pets are out there waiting for your business.

01

So, You Want to Start a Pet-Sitting Business!

Congratulations! You are considering stepping out on your own and starting a home-based pet-sitting business. If you are an animal lover, chances are you've helped a friend, family member, or coworker at some point in your life with his or her pet care needs. In fact, until just a few years ago, the term *pet sitter* meant the kid down the street or the neighbor who agreed a couple of times to put out some food and let the dog out, and you filled that need. When you helped your friend or family member, you might have thought to yourself, "This would be a great job! I wish I could do this all the time!" It's true. It can be a great job. After all, who wouldn't want to play with animals all day? But can taking care of other people's pets really generate a livable income?

The pet industry is booming. According to the American Pet Products Association, the total dollars spent on pets and their care, feeding, and well-being have doubled since 1998. In just the last five years, the industry has grown from $36.3 billion to $47.7 billion (an almost 25 percent growth). To put that into perspective, that cumulative total of $47.7 billion is more than the entire

When I started pet sitting in 1998 I never imagined our home-based business would generate enough work and income to support a family of five. I often stop and think how amazing it is that a business taking care of beloved pets can really do that! It truly amazes me. What a blessing. We grew our pet-sitting business with a small investment of a couple of hundred dollars and a book we bought online to a business employing fifteen part-time pet sitters and supporting our family comfortably. Your home-based pet-sitting business can do that, too.

revenue generated by the toy industry in America. Pet sitting falls under the "pet services" category in the pet industry, which alone accounts for over $3 billion.

In the last fifteen years, pet sitting has become a recognized profession with accreditation programs, national, regional, and local organizations, and continuing education opportunities. Our culture has come to value household pets as family members, and their comfort and care by trained, experienced, and reliable professionals are a nonnegotiable household budget item.

Several demographic, economic, and philosophical changes have led to the growth of pet sitting as a recognized and needed profession:

- Changes in community structure
- Changes in family structure
- Changes in travel reasons/patterns
- Changes in the way people view family pets

Let's take a closer look. In the fairly recent past, communities were settled by families that consisted usually of a two-parent household in which one parent worked at the same job for decades while the other parent managed the household, including caring for the family pets on a daily basis. The family members lived in the same house for many years, they knew their neighbors, and it was standard practice to ask neighbors to help care for the family pet while they were on their annual vacation. Rarely did the family members choose or need to travel together, leaving the house unattended. Business trips were conducted by the working parent, and the status quo was maintained at home. In addition, the family pet likely either stayed outside or was allowed in only certain parts of the house. It was rare to hear someone describe a pet as a "member of the family."

Looking at today's communities, you still find families like the one just described, but you also find several families, including single-parent families, new to the area. Our communities today are more dynamic, with families moving in and out more frequently. Many households consist of double-income families that work longer hours, leaving pets unattended for long hours during the day. And lastly, the average cat or dog over the last one hundred years has gone from sleeping in the barn to the back porch to the kitchen to the owner's bed. Most people these days eagerly tell you about their four-legged furry family members. They aren't just pets anymore—they are family. These are your clients.

People need you because:

- They are single and work long hours or travel frequently for work or pleasure.
- They are retired and travel frequently for pleasure.
- They are double-income couples who work long hours and need help during the day.
- They are families that enjoy frequent travel for pleasure.

Are there a market and a need for pet sitting? You bet! Can you fill that need? Is the work for you? Is running your own business for you?

People enter the professional pet-sitting field for many reasons. Some people have become discouraged with other work that seems unprofitable either emotionally or financially. Others have found their way to opening their own pet-sitting business by way of a job loss or downsizing. Still others are full-time moms and dads looking for additional income to help support the family in a way that provides flexible scheduling. Whatever the reasons are that have brought you to consider opening your own pet-sitting business, chances are you were drawn to the field because of your love for animals.

"Choose a job you love, and you will never have to work a day in your life."

—Confucius

When people ask me why or how I started pet sitting professionally, I answer, "Because I love pets and people, and I wanted to find a way to provide a service to both." I've met several would-be pet sitters who say that they want to start pet sitting because they like dealing with pets but not with people. Although it is true that the majority of your day pet sitting will be mostly you and your furry, feathered, or finned companions, it is important to truly understand how important the human owners of those companions are to your business. I have yet to have a dog or cat sign a check or give me a credit card. A natural affinity with pets is a necessity to a successful pet-sitting business, but rapport with your human clients is equally important. A pet sitter is in the pet and people business! Stop now and take an honest look at your willingness to deal every day with people from all backgrounds, with all personality types—some you probably find yourself drawn to and others with whom you won't be comfortable.

Owning your own pet-sitting business means that you have to be the sales department, the care provider, and the person who handles complaints and even collections. People skills are necessary.

My Story

I often am asked why I started Cathy's Critter Care. People will ask you, too! It is important that you be able to tell them your reasons, your history, and your story. Work on your reason "why" and have your self-promotion material ready!

Here's mine. I have an education in animal care and training—a biology degree from Texas State University with a minor in psychology. I worked my way through college in the retail field and acquired invaluable customer service training along the way. All of these things helped pave the way to success with Cathy's Critter Care.

I worked as a zookeeper at the San Antonio Zoo before I started my human family. When my first son came along in 1997, I wanted to stay at home with him and raise him, so I left the zoo. We quickly realized, though, that surviving and thriving on one income were nearly impossible. One night my husband read about the concept of professional pet sitting on the Internet. He excitedly told me the next day that he had found something he thought would be great to try and that he had bought a book on the subject. My first thought was, "How much was the book?" I read it, then I started with one client, who turned into two. Those two clients became four and so on. I honestly believe pet sitting is what I was meant to do.

My first clients were direct referrals from the two veterinarians I worked for and from local (and free) advertising I did through a local television auction. I can remember how nervous I was at my first preservice visit with my first client. My palms were sweating. She turned out to be a great client, and things went smoothly with her pet care.

My second client could meet with me only in the middle of the day, and she was leaving on short notice. This left me having to take my six-month-old son along with me to meet the client. She didn't mind and enjoyed the meeting. She and her husband were clients for numerous years until they retired and purchased an RV, and now their pets travel with them. Things have changed for me significantly since then. I probably wouldn't ask my clients if I could bring along an infant with me on a meeting. But just as my business has changed, the acceptance of pet sitting as a professional service, much like any other professional service a client can call on, has changed as well. Clients now tend to expect a more professional standard of care from their pet sitter. But that's what worked for my business then, and as I grew my business, my life and circumstances changed. Don't be afraid to make a decision based on what is right for you. There will be clients out there for you, and if you find that what you've decided doesn't seem to be working, you aren't stuck with that decision. Make changes in your structure so that you can accommodate what your clients want. That might mean researching drop-in babysitting options or hiring someone to help you.

Over the course of the years that I've been pet sitting, I would like to think I've seen just about everything and met just about every kind of person, but I am often surprised at the circumstances I encounter and the myriad people we work for. In this business you have to be ready to think on your feet in an emergency and problem solve with a sense of calm. There are probably 101 things that I could list that you might encounter, such as:

- Clients home when they're not supposed to be

- Changed locks

- Extra pets at a house

- Working for people who don't have the same housekeeping standards as you

- College-age kids home for the weekend asleep on the couch

- Bugs in pet's food

- Broken refrigerators

But with this job comes the knowledge that just when you think you've seen it all, done it all, and scooped it all, the business of pet sitting throws something new at you. That's what makes it an ever-changing and never-boring job. The fact that just about anything can happen on any given day means each day isn't the same. The best asset a person starting a home-based pet-sitting business can bring to the table is a good ability to problem solve.

If you develop the kind of relationship your clients value, not only will you be asked to pet sit for your clients, but you will also find yourself counseling them on topics from basic animal behavior issues to grief counseling, if and when they lose their beloved family pet. People will seek your input on everything from what litter to use for their new kitten to the right food to give their older pet. You might even find yourself discussing their personal problems with neighbors, their kids, and other topics not related to their pets. Your ability to listen nonjudgmentally to clients is a skill you need to bring to your business or develop through self-training. It's often a sign of trust when a client shares topics with you that you might not think pet care encompasses. You want your clients to trust you! With trust comes a natural openness that might catch you off guard. However, it is also vital to set your own boundaries with clients. You will want to remember that you have a business relationship, and your primary goal is to help care for their pets and home.

How Much Will You Make?

As with any other business endeavor, you want to make sure that you are conducting a business that makes a profit. You might not show a profit for as long as your first three years, but you will still be making money. Any business that doesn't make money for its owner is just a hobby. Although pet care and pet sitting are fun and can seem like a hobby, chances are you are looking at starting a home-based business to make money.

It's hard to estimate exactly how much any given pet-sitting business will make. Several factors determine gross and net income. Some of these are:

- Profit margin on services
- Market share
- Availability to meet client needs

Total revenue (gross revenue) − expenses = profit (net revenue)
Profit − taxes = take-home pay

I know that you want some idea of what you can make pet sitting, though, so here are some rough estimates. Keep in mind that these are averages. Pet sitting is a new industry, and unlike in other services or goods that have been around for decades, there isn't much historical data to draw from. The national average for a thirty-minute visit is about $17. But does that mean that is the price you should charge? Maybe but maybe not. With some research into your market and what your actual operating costs are, you will be able to determine the correct price for your business.

When you start pet sitting, it's not too bad on some of the busy days in the summer or around holidays when you have ten to twelve visits to do in a day. But you can't keep up that pace and last for long. You will need to allow for rest and give yourself some lighter days. The cyclical nature of pet sitting will lend itself to these downtimes during your first year in business, but be careful not to overextend yourself and run into the dreaded *b*-word: *burnout*. You can do ten to twelve visits for four to five days, but with anymore than that you run the risk of getting run down physically, emotionally, and mentally.

It is completely feasible to estimate that in your first year of pet sitting part-time you can gross between $12,000 and $20,000, depending on your location, market share, and availability. If you do not have another job, have an open market and a booming client base, and can devote more time to your business, you could see gross revenue up to $30,000. Pet-sitting businesses are growing at a quicker pace than in the past. I believe this increase is due to the fact that more people understand the concept of hiring a professional pet sitter and are seeking those services. You won't have to fight the battle as much to let people know what you do. Most pet-sitting businesses in their growth phase see about a 25 percent increase in business from year 1 to year 2 and about the same from year 2 to year 3. So, if you gross approximately $12,000 your first year, you can project grossing about $17,000 your second year. Don't forget to account for your expenses before you start banking on bringing home an extra $1,000 a month. The business plan that you put together will help you get a better grasp on what you will make after your expenses are paid.

One way to generate more income is to offer add-on services to your pet-sitting business.

Some options for your pet-sitting business include:

- Pet taxi service
- Dog training

- Cat behavior
- Errand service
- Dog party planning
- Homemade pet treats (check your health department regulations)
- Boarding at your home (be sure to check your local zoning codes and regulations)
- Trips to the dog park
- Private consultation services on pet-related topics from a new pet to dog behavior

Through Wind and Sleet and Snow

Pets have to be seen and cared for every day. They have to eat, be taken out or have their litter cleaned, and receive companionship from their caregiver. There's no staying home on your part because of an ice storm or 5 inches of rain. Pet sitters must be available to work 365 days a year in all kinds of weather and in all kinds of circumstances. There are early morning trips out in the cold of winter, midday walks in the heat of summer, and late-night care when the wind is howling and your pajamas are calling. Prepare yourself for these situations, and you will be better prepared for the hardships of the work. (In extreme circumstances, neighbors might be able to help, but you are being hired to ensure the pets are cared for appropriately. It is your responsibility to make sure that it happens.)

Can You Really Work When You Want To?

The freedom of working for yourself, when you want to, and having the ultimate in flexibility draws many people to owning their own business. Pet sitting, however, is different from many other businesses in that it requires work when most people are off from work spending time with their friends and family. Housekeepers are able to schedule cleanings on days before and after major holidays and generally don't work late into the evening. The same holds true for repair services like computer or handyman businesses. Even pet-grooming companies rarely see clients during holidays or after hours.

Unless you fill a specialized niche, pet sitting often requires work on holidays, early mornings, and late nights. When people are taking off for spring break, Easter, summer vacations, and, of course, Thanksgiving and Christmas, that's when you will be most busy. This can sometimes take a toll on your family. Be certain you have a clear understanding of these demands and that you have the important people in your life on board with your decision to pet sit professionally. As the business owner, you have the final say in whether or not you work on any specific holiday, but it is important that you realize this is primarily when you will be needed. Embrace the knowledge that you will come to love the smell of cooking turkeys as you walk dogs Thanksgiving morning. Holiday care is a necessity for almost any pet-sitting business looking to grow and thrive.

Pet sitting is cyclical in its revenue stream and client demands. Generally speaking, pet sitters are often busiest during the weeks of Thanksgiving and Christmas. Next busiest are the summer months of June, July, and August as well as spring break. Down months are January, February, and often mid- to late September (right after school starts). Keep in mind that the clients who hire you throughout the year will need your services during these busy times, and you might be picking up new clients during these busy times. There are ways to take off during a holiday occasionally, but it is not the norm. Most pet sitters choose to take their time off during their slower periods. The cyclical nature of a pet-sitting business is represented in the chart that follows. It's important to plan for your busy times by not overbooking yourself. Equally important is to set aside some of your income to help balance out the slower times.

Keep in mind that when you run your own pet-sitting business, you are the boss and that you ultimately get to decide when you take clients. There is some flexibility in what you choose to do and when, but being available when your clients need you most will prove important in building your client base enough to establish and grow your business.

Your Commute to Work

Unless you have reliable and easy-to-use public transportation, your biggest expense of time and money will be your commute. I can't stress enough the amount of driving that pet sitting involves. Obviously you will be driving from one client to the next, so prepare yourself for this inevitability. If you like books on tape, now's the time to listen. Depending on your service area, you might spend between five and twenty minutes driving from one client's home to the next. Make sure you have a vehicle that is good on gas mileage and relatively reliable. The IRS offers a mileage deduction for business travel, so keep track of the miles you drive from one client's home to the next or even to the post office to mail client invoices or to pick up your mail from your post office box.

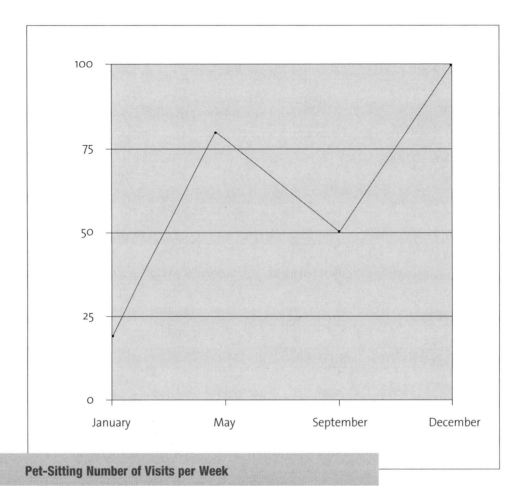

Pet-Sitting Number of Visits per Week

Your Friends' and Family's Take on Pet Sitting—Is It Worth All This?

In order for you to be successful long term as a self-employed pet sitter, a support system is absolutely necessary. If you are part of a family unit, your family has to be on board. There will be early mornings and late nights and a lot of holiday work. Inevitably at one point or another, your family members might feel like it's just not worth all of the time you have to spend away from them. They might think, or even say, things like, "Why don't you have a job where you can be at home at night?" They might resent the fact that you have to go out in the middle of Thanksgiving Day to see a family of dogs that needs to be let out. These are the real and tough situations you might be faced with. Sometimes it's difficult for those closest to us to see the

To view the current rate for mileage deduction allowed, visit www.IRS.gov. The mileage deduction changes from year to year and sometimes even within a given tax year if there are big fluctuations in the price of gas. Be sure to keep track of your miles driven for work. It is likely to be one of your biggest business expenses and deductions.

benefits of flexible scheduling. It's easy to forget how constraining a full-time job working for someone else can be.

Even today almost thirteen years after starting Cathy's Critter Care, it is hard for my kids, who are currently all school age, to understand that I am not always gone. From their perspective it seems that I am either coming or going to a pet-sitting visit and rarely at home with them. This, I assure you, isn't the case. We have ample time to go to the movies or the park. I am at almost every class party, field trip, and sporting event. Sometimes they just have to be reminded of how frequently you are there. I mention this now because having happy people around you who are on board with your home-based pet-sitting business is of vital importance to your success. To thrive long term, you will need support from the people around you. That might mean that your spouse helps you with maintaining the house, answering the phones, or even just lending a supportive ear to listen when you need to flesh out a new plan or vent about a frustrating day.

It might be a good idea when you are starting out to coordinate with another pet-sitting business owner to help with any unforeseen emergencies that happen like flat tires, the flu, or overbooked weekends. Is your mom willing to help straighten out your accounting for the month or your best friend willing to babysit for you? There will be challenges, and it is vitally important that you have some human support even if it's just a little cheerleading to keep you going.

Your spouse can be your greatest asset, as mine has been, willing to help with preparing dinners, answering phones, and juggling schedules. Spouses can also be your greatest liability if they don't see the benefit of your work. Talk over your plans with your immediate family and make sure everyone understands that even though your business is a home-based business, there will be time away throughout the day and other limitations on your time. Sometimes working for yourself requires more time away from your family than just the regular eight-hour workday. But there are other times when you have the freedom to spend a full afternoon with your family while everyone else is stuck in the humdrum of an office cubicle.

It's important for everyone in your life—friends, family, and neighbors both inside your home and out—to remember that just because you are at home doesn't mean that you aren't working.

Depending on your situation, you can set up your business to maximize your time use to least affect the family. If you have young children and a spouse or partner, you might find it beneficial to do many of your pet-sitting visits in early morning and late evening when your significant other is at home. If your children are school age, providing care throughout the day while they are away might make the most sense. With the many types of services you can offer as a professional pet sitter, you can shape your business around your needs.

Types of Services

- Once-per-day cat care
- Midday dog walking
- Overnight pet sitting
- Morning and evening pet sitting

What your business starts at might not be what it is in one year or five years. You can change your services as you need to so that they fit what you are able to do. For example, when Cathy's Critter Care started, we had one six-month-old child. I did visits in early morning before my husband left for work (I could usually fit in three visits from 5 a.m. to 7 a.m.). In the evening after he got home from work I conducted my new client meetings and evening visits. This allowed me to focus on my mom duties during the day, but I was able to start and build the pet-sitting business. Support of your marital partner is key. As the business grew, I needed to add midday care. At the time my dad was working a late-night shift, so he was able to keep my son during the day for a few hours while I tended to my pet clients. Now we have three children, all school age. So it is easier for me to focus on morning and midday care and offer my staff evening visits. Just remember that you aren't stuck in one mold of your business. Be flexible with yourself and your situation, and you can make it work.

Remember that you will need to set aside a portion of the day to complete the office part of your job, too. Don't forget to allow for office time daily. Be flexible with your business. What you can do now might change in the future, and that's okay. The best businesses change with the needs of their business and its customers.

Can Your Kids Come with You?

There are pet sitters on both sides of the fence on this question. Many successful business owners hold steadfast to never taking their kids with them pet sitting. After all, when you call a plumber or computer repair person or even a housekeeper, you don't generally see him bringing his children along. It is important to maintain the professional nature of your business, and it might send the wrong signal if you bring your children with you. Taking anyone along with you on your pet-sitting visits might also open you up to liability from the standpoint of your insurance company. You are the insured person providing care. If something happens to, or because of, someone else with you, your insurance might take issue with that. Be sure to check with your insurance provider.

When my children were smaller I found it distracting to take them with me on most of my visits. I used the services of drop-in day-care centers where the charge is hourly, not daily. I used Mother's Day Out programs at local churches, summertime high school babysitting help, and the assistance of my family members and playdates at friends' homes to help with child supervision. Think outside the box of daily child care, and you can come up with flexible options that fit your pet-sitting plan. If you have a child-care plan on set days each week, make that your time to pin down times to meet with new clients. You will want to be certain to have time available without having to scramble for child care to go meet with a new client.

For just as many successful pet sitters who never take their kids along, there are those who have not had an issue with taking their small children along either on a consistent basis or as needed during an emergency or because of a lack of child care. You will need to let your clients know of your plans to bring your child and make sure they are completely comfortable with the idea. Don't be surprised if they ask to meet your children as well as you if your children come with you. Your children are dear to you, but understand from a client's perspective that she is hiring a professional service. If she prefers that children not be brought to her home, you should respect and understand her wishes.

Make sure that you are able to focus your attention on the pets and home in your care. This might mean staying longer than your normal visit time at a house if you have to stop what you are doing with the pets to tend to your child. Ensure that your child can be with you safely. Some dogs don't like the quick movements, noises, and energy of small children. A good option is a baby backpack for very small children. This allows your hands to remain free and your child to be out of reach of the pets. A second option is a stroller that can safely confine a toddler while you work but can allow you to move the child from room to room with you or go on a walk.

It is ultimately up to you and your business plan whether or not you decide that your child can go with you. You might be able to determine from your clients' feedback if this is going to work in your area. If clients seem uneasy about your plan and use you only one time, you might need to look at bringing your children along as a possible cause.

How Much Will It Cost You To Start?

One of the most enticing things about starting a home-based pet-sitting business is the low startup costs. When I started Cathy's Critter Care in 1998, I spent $537. We had a slow computer and home Internet access, which we made do with until we had our first profitable Christmas and bought a new computer. We used our home phone line and just changed the voice mail to our business message. We really cut corners at the beginning, but it paid off. We were able to start up with minimal expense and risk and operate debt free. We waited until our third year in business to incur bigger expenses like Yellow Pages advertising and focused on grassroots advertising at minimal cost. We started with the bare bones expenses on only the

Expenses for Startup of Cathy's Critter Care 1998

Registered business in two counties—$32
Five hundred brochures—$65
Book—$30
Membership in national organization—$85
Insurance and bond—$325

necessary items, which allowed us to see a quick profit and build the business with little stress over making ends meet at the beginning. Instead of worrying about covering our expenses, we rejoiced every time we got a new client and saw a profit. There's just a different way you approach a phone call from a client when you know you are in the black on your business books. Avoid the temptation to overextend yourself in the beginning. Desperation is not a good business partner.

Do You Have the Skills and Knowledge Necessary?

Because pet owners are seeking professional care for their furry family members, they expect you to have the knowledge and expertise required of a professional. Most of your clients will give you specific directions on feeding, exercise, and medication routines that their pets are accustomed to. So, unlike computer repairs, personal chef services, or even dog training, there are minimal specialized skills you will need to have ahead of time to complete your job appropriately. Of course, the more animal knowledge you bring with you when you start your business, the better. Clients will ask you about your experience and training, so it's good to be armed with a more extensive understanding of animal care.

Taking a Pet First Aid and CPR Class Is a Necessity

The minimum pet skills/knowledge you will need are:

- Basic understanding of different dog breeds and their general characteristics
- Ability to "read" a pet's body language—especially with dogs
- Ability to visually observe animals and assess their general health
- General understanding of proper feeding of pet
- Ability to administer medications to pets of varying degrees of cooperation
- Pet first aid and CPR for emergency preparedness

To get more information on pet first aid classes you can do a quick Internet search for classes in your city or contact Pet Tech (www.pettech.net) or American Red Cross (www.redcross.org).

There are also online courses you can attend. For more information, visit www.Petco.com.

If you want to brush up on your knowledge and skills without additional out-of-pocket expense for training, you can:

- Volunteer at your local humane society/shelter to walk dogs, feed animals and clean kennels, and care for cats
- Foster a dog or cat in your home for a local rescue group
- Provide assistance to a local rescue group in transporting pets or conducting home checks
- Work with a dog trainer (provide your assistance free while you learn basic techniques)
- Fill in at a veterinarian's office part-time (this might be paid work, but you can volunteer your services in exchange for learning about medications, procedures, and basic care)
- Join a meet-up group (www.meetup.com) in your area and spend time with the people and pets in the group at meetings, hikes, and other outings

The more time you spend around animals and their owners in any capacity, the more you will refine your pet care skills with dogs and cats. Expose yourself to different pets, and you will be able to identify breeds quickly and accurately and know what characteristics are inherent in their breed. You will better understand how to correctly medicate a cat and how to spot a sick animal. Equally important, you will develop your interpersonal skills and be comfortable communicating with pet owners.

Additionally, when you join one of the national pet-sitting organizations, Pet Sitters International (PSI) or National Association of Professional Pet Sitters (NAPPS), you will have access to their accreditation courses. These are great resources to make sure you are fully equipped with the animal and business knowledge to run your home-based pet-sitting business.

Like pets, their people come with all temperaments, personalities, and motives. Want to get the scoop on dealing with all kinds of pet parents? Attend a local networking group of pet sitters. These groups are often formed around the need to talk with other people in the same field. The pet sitters at a meeting are sure to be full of stories dealing with difficult circumstances and challenging clients. You can learn from how they handled situations with successful outcomes as well as ones that didn't end so well. To find a local networking group, contact one of the national pet-sitting organizations for its official list of registered networks in your area or do an Internet search for individual pet-sitting companies. You can contact them by

The best advice I've received was, "You can please some of the people all of the time and all of the people some of the time, but you can't please all of the people all of the time." (Original quote by John Lydgate but shared with me by Dr. Leo V. Gates)

Take this advice to heart. Sometimes no matter how hard you try, you just aren't going to please everyone. It seems to be in our nature (as caring pet sitters) to focus on pleasing everyone. Although it is important to listen to honest criticism and handle complaints, try not to focus your energy on those situations. It's hard to remember that you have numerous other clients who are happy with your care, services, and pricing when you have to deal with an upset client who thinks you didn't do a good job or are overpriced. It's important to know that more often than not, if you've done your best and are consistent in your pricing, the issue might lie with the client and not you. Perhaps the client what she wanted to hear or didn't read your policies. Just don't beat yourself up over these issues when they come up. Accept the criticism, acknowledge any mistakes, but move on.

Most of our clients are happy with our rates and what we offer, but every once in awhile we talk to someone who thinks our rates are too high. "Outrageous," as one lady said. As long as you are consistently getting positive feedback and a good percentage of your clients are calling you back for care, rest assured that you are doing fine. More will be discussed later about quality client feedback tools and assessment. You have to set up your business to best suit you and the majority of your clients and know that you might not be the best fit for everyone out there.

phone or e-mail and ask them if they know of any group meetings. Although not every area has a networking group, many do. Networking groups can run the gamut from very formal structure with a president to a loose-knit group whose members get together for a quick meal and chat. Getting together with other pet sitters will give you an idea of the challenges they face on a daily basis and become a valuable resource in learning the pet-sitting trade.

The traits of a long-term pet sitter include:

- Good physical and mental health
- Good sense of humor
- Sense of responsibility

- Ability to work early mornings, late nights, and weekends
- Ability to work with people of varying personalities
- Ability to take criticism
- Flexibility with schedules and routines

The Least You Need to Know

The pet business, including pet sitting, is growing and thriving, and it is quickly becoming a recognized profession and legitimate career. Success in this career depends on the following:

- You will have to wear many hats: accountant, sales force, and customer service.
- You need to be comfortable with the fact that the buck stops with you.
- You will be your clients' advisor on many pet-related issues encompassing more than just pet sitting.
- Earning a comfortable part-time income and growing it into a full-time income are possible.
- Add-on services like pet taxi and dog parties can help increase your income.
- You must be in good physical and mental health to pet sit.
- Be prepared to work in all kinds of weather, on weekends and holidays.
- Understand that pet sitting is cyclical in nature with busy months and slow months.
- Pet sitting involves a lot of driving—a reliable vehicle is a necessity.
- The support of your family and friends and even other pet sitters is crucial to keeping you in business long term.
- Be flexible with your business and willing to change if necessary to accommodate your needs or the needs of your clients.

Action Steps

- Talk with your family members to ensure that they are supportive and on board with your business idea.
- Have your vehicle checked to make sure it is reliable and in good working order.
- Sign up for pet first aid/CPR classes.
- If you believe you are in need of additional hands-on training, volunteer with a local shelter or with a dog trainer.

02

Envisioning the Business
Painting the Full Picture of What Your Pet-sitting Business Will Look Like

You probably have some idea in your mind of the work you will be doing, your service area, business name, the type of pets you will be caring for, and possibly even some of the details like where you might set up your home office. This is fun and exciting when you think about your new venture. Let's take some time to finish painting the picture of your business.

Where Will You Provide Pet Sitting?

Most home-based pet sitters provide care in a 5–15-mile radius from their home. This service area is going to be dictated in part by the number of potential clients you have in that area. For example, if you live in a rural area and will be focusing your care there, you might need to expand your service area to a larger radius. If you live in a densely populated area of affluent-income homes, you might be able to provide your services in as small an area as a few neighborhoods. I know of one Houston, Texas–based pet sitter that provides care only to her neighborhood and has grown her business to a very comfortable income. Ultimately it is up to you and the number of clients and visits you anticipate doing. Take a look at a map of your area. Write down the neighborhoods, cities, and/or zip codes in which you anticipate providing your pet-sitting services. From this list you can determine who else is in your potential market area. Don't worry too much about selecting too small or too large an area. You can modify your service area as needed to increase or decrease your work if need be. A good starting point for most home-based suburban pet-sitting businesses is a service area radius of 10 miles.

Your First Step—Determine a Need in Your Area

You might have some idea of what you can and should charge for your services. The national average for a standard thirty-minute pet-sitting visit is about $17, but the rates range from between $12 and $22, depending on location and cost of living. Maybe you or a friend have used one of the pet-sitting businesses in your area already. Many people have a good idea of just about what the going rate is for their particular area and what services they offer, but when any business enters the marketplace it is wise to do some research on which companies are already providing the goods or services that the new business plans to provide as well. It is required research to position yourself appropriately in your market. It's such an important part of starting a business that market research is a section of any complete business plan. If you haven't already done so, now is the time to take a serious look at who is out there already and what services they are offering. Set up a simple table like the following one to keep track of what you find. You will use this information later when you build your business plan, so take notes. You will likely find at least one person in your area offering pet sitting. You might find several established businesses. That's okay. On the other hand, if you don't find anyone listed in your potential service area, you might need to rely on pet sitters from other cities or use the national average as a good starting point for your rates.

Find Area Businesses Using This List

Business Name and Owner's Name	Web Address	Phone Numbers	Service Area	Service and Rates	Additional Note

- Printed Yellow Pages (*NOTE:* there might be several brands of business phone books out there, so locate the different copies and versions from all of the businesses that print and distribute them)
- Online business pages (www.yellowpages.com, www.yellowbook.com, www.superpages.com, www.realpageslive.com, www.dexknows.com)

- Online service area zip code or city at www.petsit.com, www.petsitters.org, www.petsitusa.com
- Google search of "pet sitter" with the zip code(s) of your potential service area and/or the city name.
- Call to local veterinarians and groomers to ask if they know of any local pet sitters.

Doing this should get you a good list of all the pet-sitting businesses in your area. Now that you know who is out there providing pet care, look at their websites for the following information:

- Types of pets cared for—dogs, cats, livestock, exotics
- Services offered—visit length, overnight care, dog running, visits to dog parks, care in pet sitter's home

Service Areas

If a pet-sitting business does not have a website, and you still feel that you need more market input, you can call the business and introduce yourself as a potential new business. There's no need to pretend to be a client. Most pet sitters know what's going on with the questions asked on calls and will realize that your questions are from someone interested in starting a business, not booking care. If you are honest up front, they will appreciate your honesty, and you won't have to pretend to be something you are not. It is more comfortable for everyone if you are clear about the intentions of your call. The majority of pet sitters will be willing to talk with you. Most pet sitters are genuinely nice people who are more concerned with what is best for pets and their people than driven by a need to be the only successful business in an area. They may or may not be completely open to sharing their rates or policies with you directly, but you probably have a good idea from the online businesses what those rates are in your area. Should you come across people who seem unwilling to talk with you, simply thank them for answering and wish them well. You can expect to get voice mail quite a bit, too. Many pet sitters are out pet sitting and handle their phone calls when they get back home. Be prepared to concisely state who you are and your reason for calling should you get voice mail. Ask that sitters call you back at a time convenient for them and be ready for the phone call.

Be respectful of the business owners' time. Generally keeping your phone call to under five minutes should be your goal. Try to do more listening than talking.

> ### Potential Script for Phone Call to Pet-Sitting Business
>
> Hi. My name is Cathy. I found your information in the Yellow Pages and wanted to talk with you about your business. However, I am not a potential client but rather am looking at starting my own pet-sitting business. Could I talk with you for just a minute or two? I know you are probably very busy. [Pause and listen. If you get the go-ahead, continue.] Thank you very much. I appreciate it. Do you know of any local pet-sitter networks? [Pause and listen. Take notes.] In what areas of town do you provide care? [Pause and listen.] Would you mind sharing with me what the general rate for a regular visit is and in general if you have any tips for a new sitter? [Pause and listen.] Thank you for your time. I really appreciate it. I am excited to get started and would be happy to refer clients I can't help back to you. Would it be okay if I called you in the future if I have another question? Thanks. Bye.

After all, you placed the call to gain information from them. Listen to what they have to say. At the end of the conversation, thank them for taking time to talk with you and ask them if they would be open to your calling another time in the future if questions come up. If you've kept your call brief and your questions pertinent, they shouldn't have a problem with a future call.

If you are in an area that doesn't currently have any professional pet-sitting services, you will have to research markets similar to yours but in a different locale. It's definitely better to know that you've researched the pricing and services that you offer than to just guess at what might work. You will be better off knowing for yourself that you are within the realm of normalcy for services and pricing.

Eventually you will get a phone call from someone looking for services that you don't offer or someone who disagrees with your pricing. Don't let these people knock you off course. If you've done your research into other companies in your area or in markets similar to yours, you can rest assured and confidently convey that your pricing is in line with the industry. I've had people tell me that my prices are "insulting, ridiculous, and even criminal." It goes back to serving well those people whom you can but not being hung up on pleasing all the people all the time. Another great way to get many of these questions answered is to attend one or more of the annual pet-sitting conventions put on by the national or regional professional organizations. For more information on the conventions held by Pet Sitters International and National Association of Professional Pet Sitters, visit their websites. These conventions are invaluable resources for asking questions. Everyone comes to the convention ready to share ideas, talk, and inspire each other. Each year numerous people at the conventions are just looking into starting a pet-sitting business. Those new folks are balanced out by the seasoned sitters who've been in business for several years and attended many conventions. Conventions are generally held once a year in January or February.

Regional and local meetings are held at other times of the year as well. If you've missed the annual convention, look into one of the smaller meetings. You might find that one is planned soon and within a good traveling distance. It's of great benefit to go.

However, if you cannot find a national, regional, or local meeting, don't let that keep you from getting your home-based pet-sitting business off the ground today. If you've done your market research for your area, you will be on the right track.

Where Do You Fit In?

Do the people and pets in your area even need a pet sitter if established companies already provide this service? Why bother starting a pet-sitting business if existing businesses are already doing well? Even in areas where several pet-sitting businesses are set up, there is still a need for new choices for clients. With more than half the households in America now owning pets and the growing philosophy that pets are members of the family that deserve the best care we can give them, you have a good potential client base, and there are enough pet owners to market your business to. If you can work with the pet-sitting companies that are already in existence in a mutually beneficial way, you will find that there are plenty of clients out there.

Most people fear competition. Have you heard the saying, "Competition is healthy"? Aron Rosenberg, cofounder and chief technology officer for SightSpeed, puts this into tangible terms for business. "Competition is very healthy for our business. One of the things that we found was that we used to be afraid of when a competitor would enter the marketplace with a new product. What generally happens is that, when a competitor comes into the marketplace, it brings attention to it. That attention is good for everybody. Owning 90 percent of a one hundred-person market is meaningless if you can own 1 percent of a one billion-person market, and so having more people involved in your industry means that that industry is getting bigger and so the piece of the pie, the total pie has to be bigger, which is better for everybody involved."

Embrace your competition both figuratively and literally. Attend networking meetings, make phone calls to other pet sitters, and get to know them. Mutually referring clients back and forth will become a great strength for your business and theirs.

Calling All Dogs and Cats? Will You Specialize or Be a Jack-of-All-Trades?

One of the best things about starting a pet-sitting business is the ability to choose the services and types of pets you want to care for. Keep in mind, though, that the more you limit yourself at the beginning, the smaller your market of clients will be. If you feel comfortable taking care of a wide variety of pets, and you want to grow your pet-sitting business, then start out offering a variety of services to a variety of pets. The defining question you need to ask yourself when determining the types of pets you will take care of is this: Ultimately how big do you want to grow your business and how fast? If your goal is to grow to a point as quickly as possible or to grow your business as big as possible, then you will need to open up your client base to encompass as many pet species and offer as many service options as possible. That doesn't mean that you will need to do that for the life of your business, but the

You don't want to make yourself too exclusive at the beginning of your business because your market share might be too small to allow you to grow. You can always cut back later and start focusing more on the types of pets and visits you are more drawn to. Keep in mind that the more types of services you can provide and the more types of pets you are comfortable caring for, the faster you will be able to establish a good client base and get your business growing. Don't shortchange yourself. If you don't have medical or physical limitations in caring for animals, by asking the right questions of the client, you will be able to adequately care for just about any type of pet or even livestock animals. Don't go in uneducated by any means. Do your research and ask the client questions, and you can open up doors to other options for your business. Some areas like horse care, specialized grooming, and styling or veterinary hospice care might require additional training but might be worth it if the need is apparent in your area.

more people you can help in the beginning, the faster you will establish yourself in the market, start making money, and get referrals. By no means should you care for pets that you are not fully prepared to through your experience and training. If you are comfortable dealing with big dogs, for example, but prefer to take care of cats, then open yourself up to say "yes" to those folks with big dogs when you start out. If, however, you are allergic to cats or not physically capable of dealing with long walks with large dogs or are afraid of dealing with birds, then you can tailor your business to provide care only in the manner to which you are best suited.

Pet Care Options

- Cat-only care—feline specialist
- Dog-only care—canine specialist
- Small dog-only care
- Bird care
- Reptile and amphibian care
- Exotic care
- Livestock and farm animal care

Service Options

- Full-service vacation care with visits daily to the home (most pet-sitting companies offer between one and four visits daily, with the average visit being about thirty minutes)
- Overnight care in which the pet sitter spends the night in the home
- Twenty-four-hour care in which the pet sitter stays at the home day and night while the owners are gone (possibilities include pet sitter being able to leave for short times to attend to other clients with scheduled visits but is primarily at the owner's home during the day as well as night)
- Special-needs pets (paraplegic pets, insulin-dependent pets)
- Veterinary hospice care (end-of-life care for pets)
- Care for clients in hotels/RV parks, etc. while they are in your town. Care might include staying in the room with a pet who has separation anxiety, or it might just be for a dog walk.
- Pet taxi service to transport animals
- Pet care/doggy day care in your home
- Trips to dog parks

- Dog running
- Dog training/behavior modification
- Pooper scooping service
- Midday dog walks for busy professionals
- Grooming (from basic bathing to full-service clipping and styling)

As you can see, there are many opportunities to meet clients' needs and many ways for you to fill a niche if you choose to do so. Of course, your market will drive some of your decisions. If you live in an urban area you probably won't get many calls for farm animal care. Likewise, if you live in the middle of a rural county, midday dog walking and trips to a dog park might not be where you find most of your clients. So think about your clients' needs logically and think about all of those needs you might be able to meet.

Many businesses have succeeded by specializing in cat care only. Although it limits your market share, it can help set you apart from other pet sitters in your area, and many cat owners find it reassuring that their pet sitter is a cat specialist. Whether it is the idea that their cats won't be subjected to smelling the scents of dogs on the pet sitter or that the cat sitter focuses all of her attention on the care, health, and well-being of felines isn't clear or consistent, but many cat-only businesses thrive. Determine your service area.

Your Service Area

The bigger your service area, the more customers you will have in your market area and the faster your business will grow. You should consider some definite logistical issues when selecting your service area. I've seen businesses start out offering care in a 50-mile radius. Although you are opening yourself up to a huge market, that is probably too much area to cover. After you factor in your cost in transportation and your travel time, you might be working for free. Consider those things when determining what your service area will be. Most startup pet-sitting companies are comfortable with a 10–15-mile radius. Is this right for you? Look at some online maps and see how far that puts you away from home. Keep in mind that if you take a client 15 miles from you, that might be your only client in that direction. Determine if that is cost-effective for you.

Sometimes rural pet sitters have to open up to driving even farther than the suburban pet sitter because there just aren't enough clients located together

A couple of great resource sites for demographic research are:

www.city-data.com

www.factfinder.census.gov

geographically. If you are a rural pet sitter, keep this in mind and be sure to allow for longer driving distances in your pricing structure.

Urban pet sitters can often limit their geographic range to a small area because a high number of people (and thus pets) reside geographically close by. It's not unheard of for a downtown pet-sitting service to provide care in one zip code only. Each city and situation is different, so research the demographics for your area.

Will You Work Part-Time or Full-Time?

Unless you've been pet sitting in a nonprofessional capacity already and have some established clients already, your business will dictate this question. Startup pet-sitting companies will generate an income and hours considered part-time for the infancy of their business and likely through the first year. It will take you time to establish your client base such that you can work full-time if you desire. That's okay. It takes some time to get comfortable with your new pet-sitting schedule. Don't worry about being only part-time at first. You will want to get your feet wet and get comfortable with your new business. Too much too fast might sabotage the overall game plan.

How much time it takes for your business to grow to the level of full-time will depend on several factors, including:

- The number of clients needing your services in your proposed service area
- Your availability to serve clients' varying needs
- Your ability to establish yourself in the market

If you've already been pet sitting for friends and family, you might have a good base for referrals and be able to start out quickly on the road to a full-time pet-sitting job.

Beware! Pet sitting is a demanding profession physically, emotionally, and mentally. It's often hard to continue to pet sit full-time on your own without capable support staff. Whether you hire people to help you with visits or to help you with the office tasks will be up to you. But many pet sitters have let themselves reach the point of burnout by trying to work their pet sitting job full-time all the time.

Is a Franchise for You?

If the idea of starting your own home-based pet-sitting business from the ground up intimidates you, perhaps the idea of buying into a franchise is an option. The idea of franchising a business is a relatively new concept in the business world. What could widely be argued as the most popular franchise, McDonald's restaurants, sold its first franchise opportunity in 1955. When you purchase a franchised business, you are buying a system for doing business, a territory in which that business may be conducted, and the name recognition of that business. There are several pet-sitting franchises, and each has its own set of guidelines and options on the support it offers new franchisees and costs associated with a franchise.

One of the major benefits of buying into a franchise is that you obtain a system for doing business as a pet sitter. Most franchises offer the business owner many essential forms, training, instruction, and sometimes mentoring in starting a home-based pet-sitting business. You will likely obtain quick access to vendors of other services like online booking systems, background check companies, and even a list of accountants or other professional services that are accustomed to handling the specific issues that arise for a pet-sitting business.

In addition, you are purchasing the right to use the franchise name. This is important for name recognition. Think about your favorite fast food places, casual dining restaurants, and even businesses like tax preparation services. When you are in a different town, it's likely that you see the same places. These are franchises. They count on the fact that you've been to another franchise location, you recognize the name, logo, and storefront, and you will thus come to their business because you are familiar with their product, pricing, and service. Franchises have a consistent format that customers can expect to experience no matter which franchise location they visit. This same concept is applied to pet-sitting franchises.

> Research a pet-sitting franchise by doing a quick Internet search for "franchise pet sitting." New franchise opportunities are popping up frequently.

When you agree to become a franchisee, there are sometimes limitations on how you run your business and even the areas in which you can conduct your pet sitting. In exchange for agreeing to conduct your business in accordance with the franchise rules, the franchisor will guarantee you that no other franchise from that company will be permitted to operate in your area. However, this does not limit other pet-sitting companies from working in that territory. You will still have competition from individual home-based pet-sitting companies and perhaps other pet-sitting franchise companies.

Franchises do not guarantee your personal success with your business. They get you headed in the right direction through a tested method or system for a business and sometimes offer support and additional training.

In my opinion, pet sitting does not necessarily lend itself to the franchise concept as easily as other businesses. Pet sitting is a very personal business. Your clients are going to hire you, come back to you, and refer you to their friends and neighbors because they feel comfortable with you. If someone has hired a pet sitter before from a franchise in another location and moves to where you are, unless he is comfortable with you, he will still have other options. When a client hires a pet sitter, she is hiring that person to care for her pets. She is not as interested in maintaining a system of business as she is in hiring someone with whom she is personally comfortable and who has the knowledge necessary to care for her pets. If you are reading this book, you are doing the research necessary to set up your own successful method for starting and running your home-based pet-sitting business.

On the other hand, purchasing a franchise might be right for you. If you investigate a franchise that suits your style of business and that you are interested in owning, then doing so from the beginning can be the smart choice. You can assure yourself a market of clients close to your home and protect your area from another franchisee's purchase (from that same franchisor). The key to finding a good franchise is knowing that the benefits of owning a franchise outweigh the drawbacks.

Benefits will include:

- A system of running the business
- Vendor relationships for accounting, scheduling, supplies
- Regional or nationwide advertising and marketing

Some of the drawbacks are:

- Upfront costs of purchasing the franchise
- Continuing costs in revenue percentages and other areas
- Limited accessibility to other markets already owned by another franchisee from the same franchise
- Limiting factors on how you may actually conduct your business under the franchise

Sole Proprietor, Partnership, LLC (Limited Liability Corporation), LLP (Limited Liability Partnership), or Inc.?

The conditions, exclusions, taxing, and liability obligations involved in the legal structure of your business are complicated and cumbersome to understand and decipher at best. The laws are continuously changing. Some research on your part will be in order to determine what the best fit for your business will be, and the advice of an attorney or CPA can be valuable in this area if you're not certain about what is best for you and your business. You can also talk with your local Small Business Administration office or a SCORE mentor for their advice. Each state can vary in its requirements and dealings with LLCs and incorporations, so make sure any advice you receive pertains to your particular state and circumstances.

Each website also offers free online workshops that are easy to understand, short, and self-paced. The SBA site even offers printable certificates of completion—a

Don't be afraid to ask for help.
Two valuable resources for help from professionals who are happy to give advice are:
www.score.org
www.sba.org

valuable resource to your presentation book. Score offers online webinars from industry leaders and experts that you can download and listen to at your convenience. Some of the workshops include advice and lessons on:

- Business planning
- Marketing and staying competitive
- Considering legal issues for your business
- Growing your business
- Managing cash flow and other finances

There is no right or wrong answer for what is the best approach to setting up a pet-sitting business' legal structure. What might be right for one business may not be the case for another. Some pet-sitting businesses conduct business in multiple states, and others are limited to just one community. Some businesses are run by several partners and others by a single person. The best choice for your business will depend on your individual answers to some business questions and your circumstances. I will outline the basics of each choice so that you can begin to determine the right direction for your business.

The Sole Proprietor

Sole proprietorship is enticing for most startup home-based businesses because it is easy to get started and requires minimal paperwork, filings, and fees. The sole proprietor and the business he is conducting either through his own name or through his filed dba (doing business as) name are considered one and the same. The business is the owner, and the owner is the business. Taxes are paid directly as individual income on profit and on the individual's personal tax return.

There are two major drawbacks to the sole proprietorship. The first is that any personal assets are open to collection by creditors for debts or for liability in legal obligations. If you have a personal savings account or equity in your home or other assets, these may be used to pay creditors or settle lawsuits. There essentially is no separation between what you owe/own and what the business owes/owns. This can be a scary scenario, but generally speaking, the individual pet sitter, working alone, with good business insurance including a sound care, custody, and control policy is not open to a huge amount of liability. However, use caution if you have substantial assets because they will be open to anyone winning a lawsuit against you that is not covered by your insurance policy. The second drawback is that the business, because it is tied to an individual, ceases to exist should permanent disability or death occur to the business owner. If you foresee your small business continuing should something happen to you, keep in mind that the sole proprietorship option might not be the best for you.

If you are not worried about assets or liability when you start your business, you can begin as a sole proprietorship. Then, as circumstances change—for example, you hire employees—you can change your business to another structure with less exposure to risk.

Partnerships—General and Limited

There are two types of partnerships: general and limited. General partnerships give equal responsibility, investment, and business involvement to all parties. Limited partnerships limit the amount of liability to the limited partner for an amount up to her investment in the business. However, the limited partner has no say in any of the business dealings.

Partnerships can be tricky. Have solid partnerships worked before? Yes. Some even long term. But what starts as a friendship or business partnership with the best of intentions can lead to disaster, too. A general partnership has the same legal and tax implications as a sole proprietorship but with two or more people involved. So each partner's personal assets stand for the business as well. This can be a bad situation if one partner in an agreement makes bad, or even unethical, decisions that impact the business. In the case of general partnerships, all partners in the business will be held liable through business and personal assets for anything that any of the partners does to impact the business.

Incorporating

A corporation is considered a separate legal entity from the individual(s) who make up that corporation. Therefore, there is protection from liability through lawsuits and creditors. However, in most states there is a formal process you must go through to form a corporation.

You must:

- File articles or certificate of incorporation at your state capital
- Elect a board of directors
- Adopt bylaws
- Choose officers

There are some tax differences between corporations and other legal business structures. Taxes are filed on the corporation profits, and usually payments are made in the form of salaries paid to the corporation employees.

Very few home-based pet-sitting businesses have seen the need to incorporate their business.

The Limited Liability Corporation

The LLC has become a popular way to receive many of the benefits of the sole proprietorship and the security of incorporation. LLCs are relatively easy to set up but do require filing a certificate with the secretary of state. The owners of the LLC (one or more) are taxed on the profits of the LLC on their personal tax return, making filing easier than with a corporation. However, the major benefit of the LLC is that only the assets owned by the LLC are subject to liability. This removes a huge burden from the small business owner. In addition, the LLC has rights of survivorship like those of a corporation should something catastrophic happen to you.

If the LLC seems right for your business, be sure to:

Always conduct business in the name of the LLC and include LLC on your printed materials

Never commingle business and personal funds

Be sure your LLC is registered before conducting any business transactions

Choosing Your Name . . . and Making Sure Nobody Else Has!

Shakespeare said, "What's in a name?" As any business owner knows, the answer to that is, "everything is in a name" when it comes to your business. The business name will become the business identity and the most frequently encountered part of your business (outside of your smiling face and cheerful voice). It's important to choose your business name wisely. Your business name will speak for you when it's on your business card or viewed in the phone book.

Choosing a business name is a huge task. You want your company to stand out with a memorable name. It might be catchy and cute or businesslike, but it needs to be memorable. Part of your marketing later will involve making your business name something people remember, but having a solid name to start with makes that task even easier. With pet sitting, you will want to gear your name toward something that generates a warm and comfortable feeling. Choosing your business name is one of the most important decisions you will make when planning your business and the one with the most exceptions to the rules on what works and what doesn't.

Many of the business names stemming from commonly used pet words have already been used and lack the originality they once had. When pet sitting as a profession started a little more than twenty years ago, fun names that played on words were new and unique. That's not the case now that there are tens of thousands of registered businesses with the two major national pet-sitting organizations.

As you think about your business name, write down several options that come to mind. Brainstorm and as you think of other names in the car or in the shower (which are the two places I do my best thinking), add them to your list. What might seem like the best choice to you might not be what works when some of your trusted friends look at your choices. These friends will serve as your test group.

Ideally you want to choose a name that is unique, catchy, and easily remembered while conveying what your business does but without limiting your business identity too much to pin you into one corner of a market. In addition, pet sitting is a personal business, so you need your business name to convey some sort of emotional response from the person who encounters your business name but not excessively cute if that's not the business identity you are looking for. Conversely, your personal pet-sitting business can't afford to leave a first impression of feeling cold or impersonal. Look for a name that gives a feeling of warmth and a personal connection. Think about some words that convey that feeling.

Generally speaking, try to avoid using your personal name in the business. You might grow fast, have a great business model, and be ready to franchise your business, but it will be tied to your name. That was the mistake I made. If I had had this book, perhaps I wouldn't have named my business "Cathy's Critter Care." In addition, sometimes people think I am a child-care provider. I have yet to understand people who call their human children "critters," but I've run into several. Over the course of my twelve years in business, I've thought of many other business names that probably would have worked better for me. But don't let the options stop you from proceeding. Despite my not-so-perfect business name, "Cathy's Critter Care" has done fine, and your business will, too.

Consider carefully the following before choosing your business name:

- Including your personal name
- Including any words or phrases that might be offensive or misconstrued
- Including a geographic limiter like a city name
- Being too generic and not letting people know that you are in the pet-care field
- Using colloquialisms or foreign words that might not be widely understood

I know of a couple of pet sitters who have absolutely no intention of ever hiring anyone to work in their pet-sitting business and want to stay small and have their business name identify them personally. In that instance, having their personal name in the business name works well for them. If you are Suzie Jane, and your business is Suzie Jane's Pet Sitting and Home Care, the chances of someone else already having that name or confusing you with another business are very low.

I've seen the use of a nickname work well in naming a business. Donna Naylor in San Antonio, Texas, chose "Blondie's Pet Care" as her business name. It is memorable and associated with Donna. It's not likely that anyone else would want to call her business "Blondie's Pet Care" because she probably doesn't have an association with the word "Blondie." And "Blondie" doesn't pen her into just her name alone. "Blondie" could be anyone. If you have a great nickname, consider using that.

If you choose a common word associated with pets or sitting, the chances of your clients getting you mixed up with someone else and calling the wrong person might become an issue. You can avoid confusion by keeping in touch with your clients through marketing, advertising, and communication efforts (more on that later in the book). But distinguishing between which "Tails" business Coco liked so much last time or which company their friend referred them to might become confusing to clients when they open the phone book, and there are multiple business names with the word *tail* in them (or *paw, critter, fur,* or any of the others listed below).

It's also good to avoid using a geographically limiting word in your business

Some Common Words in Pet-Sitting Names

Paw/Paws/Pawsitive	Wag/Wags/Wagging/
Pawprints	Waggin'
Pals	Pamper/Pampered
Pet/Pets	Sitting
Sit/Sitters	Whiskers
Cute	Tails
Reliable	Professional
Reigning	Happy
Critter	Park
Feathers	Run
Fin	Luv/Love/Loved
Bone	Care
Home	Creature
Come	Nanny
People	Biscuit
Fur/Furry	Stay
Play	

name like your neighborhood, town, or city name. Although it describes your service area, it might be too limiting for you in the future. You might want to encompass an area that's not currently in the city. You might want to expand, or you might even move. You will want to use the name you have worked so hard to establish. So naming your business "Clarksville Pet Sitting" won't do you any good if you move to Meyerstown or decide to provide care to Meyerstown. Don't limit yourself when you are starting. You never know where this business will take you.

Be careful not to cross the line in choosing your words. What might seem a cute pun at the time can convey the wrong message to someone. Perception is reality when you are marketing your business, so use caution and avoid inappropriate puns in your name. Have numerous friends and trusted family members look at your choice of business name and ask them to write down their thoughts about it. Is it appropriate? What images come to mind for them? They need to be honest with you, so encourage them to do so. Now is the time to find out if your business name works. Try to get feedback from a minimum of ten to fifteen honest people. They will be your test group.

Select three to five business names that you like. Give each of your test group participants index cards with one of the names you are considering written on each card. Each business name should have its own card. Ask members of your test group to do two things:

- Brainstorm and write down on each index card all of their first thoughts that the business name brings to mind. Ask them not to filter their responses. When it comes to mind, write it down. Let them remain anonymous and tell them to be honest.
- Rank the names in order of their preference first to last.

Be cautious if you are considering any foreign words or colloquial phrases. They might not be understood by the average person or someone new to your area who isn't familiar with the words.

So where does that leave you if you shouldn't use your name or the area you will service or any of the associated words that deal with pets? Can we even name a pet-sitting business at this point? Of course. If you decide to use your name or your city in your business name, that's okay. Just think about what you want from your business, and that will lead you in the right direction.

Making Sure You Can Use the Name!

Obviously you don't want to choose any names of pet-sitting businesses already operating in your area. You should have a good idea of the business names already taken in your area from doing your previous market research. In addition, you probably want to avoid closely related names in other pet-sitting industry businesses like groomers and dog trainers. Although these people can be great assets to your business for mutual referrals and networking opportunities, you don't want to constantly have to explain to people calling you that they have the wrong business, and conversely you don't want to miss out on business because they've called the wrong place.

After you've selected your favorite (and best-received) business name, it's time to make sure nobody else already has that name and that you have the legal right to use it. This will take some research on your part, but thanks to the Internet, that process is much easier than in the past.

Start your search by simply typing your proposed business name(s) into your favorite search engine. Search through the links you get and see if anyone else is already using that business name—especially in your state and local vicinity. In addition you definitely want to look for any franchise names that have been taken already. Unless you have chosen an unusual or unique name, chances are there might be another business already using that name. But don't panic. Just because there is a business in another state using the same name you've chosen doesn't mean you can't use it. In addition, if a business provides service in a different class or section of business than your pet-sitting business, you can still likely use the name you've chosen. Use caution in that aspect, though. Even though you wouldn't be in the same service class, you want to stay away from using what's known as a "strong trademark." For example, choosing "Coca-Cola Pet Sitting" for your business name will probable draw unwanted attention. However, choosing a name that isn't as widely known or as strong a mark and is in a different class than your pet-sitting business would still be fine.

After you've done a thorough general Internet search, you can check for federal service marks at the federal trademark website: www.uspto.gov. The site has an easily searchable format.

Most people are familiar with trademarking a business logo or name, but did you know that the term for marking a pet-sitting business is service marking? Businesses that sell tangible items receive trademarks. Businesses that provide services receive service marks. The two terms have become interchangeable, and some businesses encompass both tangible items as well as service. Think about McDonald's restaurants. They serve food that is trademarked but provide food service that is service marked.

Generally speaking, there are three levels of registration for a business. It is wise to check all levels of registration before proceeding further with your business name.

- Registering your business at the local/county level
- Service marking your business with the state
- Service marking your business with a federal mark

As you can tell, trademarking and service marking are complicated issues sometimes requiring legal guidance, direction, and advice. The last thing you want to have to do when opening and running your home-based pet-sitting business is fight a legal battle over the right to use your business name. It's never fun to get a cease-and-desist letter in the mail. You can hire a law firm specializing in trademarks to conduct a search for you. Prices for the search will range from $100 to $750 depending on the extent of the search of your name availability. Some services include the registration of the mark for your business.

Lastly, you will need to check the availability in your county of the name you've chosen. Some counties require that you go to their office to conduct the search. However, more counties are updating their records to include online data in easily searchable formats. Either way, you must ensure that your business name is unique in your county and that the name can be registered to you. Someone might have registered the business name but not be anywhere on the Internet or in the phone book, so be sure you don't skip this step.

After you've completed the research on your proposed business names and found them to be clear of local use, state service mark, and federal trademark, then

Businesses can receive federal trademarks and service marks only if they sell products or provide services in more than one state. Generally your home-based business will need to register only in the county and apply for a state service mark. Because franchises operate in multiple states, most franchise names have a federal trademark making it an infringement to use that name or anything closely related and easily confused with that name.

you can register your business in the county where you will conduct business. Most counties require that businesses register their business name and pay a nominal fee. Usually your registration and fee are good for several years.

Each county is different, so when you call your county office, ask these questions:

> To locate your county office information, www.naco.org will get you the information you need quickly.

- Is this the right place to register a new business and obtain a dba (doing business as)?
- How do I check for business name availability?
- How much is the registration fee?
- How long is the registration valid?

A Quirky Rule!

Most states require that you use your business name and logo before you apply for a state service mark. This is a step you will have to wait to do until a later date, but when you have been in business for a short time, you can find the forms necessary to register for a state service mark through the secretary of state. Usually a quick search engine query will get you to the site for your secretary of state. By receiving your service mark for your business on the state level, you are protected against anybody else in your state opening a new business under your name, and it is significantly cheaper than federal trademarks. Don't forget to follow through on this step later.

Last But Not Least—Your Web Domain Name

You've selected your business name. Nobody else is using it or has it registered in at least your county. You've verified there is no state service mark or federal mark. Now check online (the easiest spot is www.register.com, whether or not you choose to purchase the name through that site). Enter your proposed business name and click "Search." If your proposed domain name is already registered by someone else, try variations by adding a hyphen or another way to make your domain name unique. The site will give you suggestions as well. Don't get too complicated with underscores, and stay away from the suffix *.net*, *.biz*, and *.us*. Most people are accustomed to the suffffix *.com*, so try to find an unregistered name with that suffix. If you've already registered with the county, and you find an Internet domain name available, purchase it through any of the online sites offering that service.

The Least You Need to Know

- Most startup home-based pet-sitters provide care in a 10–15-mile radius of their home.
- Study your competition by researching who is in the pet-sitting business now, what services they provide, and what prices they charge.
- National conventions are worth attending and are held in January and February.
- Local networking groups are invaluable to new pet sitters. Find a group by asking other pet sitters. If there isn't one, start one.
- Determine what animals you will take care of and what services you will provide. The more diverse you can be, the faster you will grow.
- Home-based pet-sitting businesses start out as part-time work but will grow into a full-time income if desired. By the end of your first year you can expect to have forty to eighty clients who have used your services.
- Franchise opportunities are available for pet-sitting businesses.
- Choosing your name is one of the most important things you will have to do before opening your business. Choose wisely.
- You must register your business name at least at the county level.

Action Steps

- Make a list of all pet-sitting businesses listed in the Yellow Pages directory and for your zip code(s) online at www.petsit.com, www.petsitters.org, and www.petsitusa.com.
- Research the businesses on your list by reviewing their websites for services and pricing.
- Check with Pet Sitters International (www.petsit.com) and National Association of Professional Pet Sitters (www.petsitters.org) for any registered local networking groups in your area.

- Choose three to five business names that are well received by your friends and family.
- Research your chosen names online and make sure you are clear to use one of them.
- Register your name with the county office.
- Purchase your domain name online.

03

Your Home Office and Mobile Office

One of the most enticing aspects of setting up a home-based pet-sitting business is the flexibility of your office space. If you are limited in space, the good news is that you don't need much room for a home-based pet-sitting business. You don't have inventory to keep on hand or need space to kennel pets. The majority of your work in your home office will be answering your client calls, checking e-mails, and booking visits. You will need to store some of your client files and possibly keys and do some basic accounting work. But other than that, your work will be off-site.

Your Home Office

What you do from home will dictate what you need for your office:

- Answering your phone
- Booking clients
- Checking e-mails
- Mapping routes to clients' homes
- Accounting

Most of your duties for booking clients through phone or e-mail, mapping, and even accounting can be conducted on a home computer. You can even opt for a laptop computer, making this component as mobile as you are.

You don't have to invest in a huge filing cabinet to safely store your client files. Portable storage boxes will work fine for at least your first year in business and are convenient and easily put into a locking safe.

Generally, to claim a business deduction for your home, you must use part of your home exclusively and regularly

- as your principal place of business; or

- as a place to meet or deal with patients, clients, or customers in the normal course of your business; or

- in any connection with your trade or business where the business portion of your home is a separate structure not attached to your home. For more details visit www.IRS.gov.

Internet service providers offer wi-fi connections for your computer at a reasonable monthly price. With a laptop and cell phone, your office can be just about wherever you are. You will still have to set aside a space to store paper/hard copies of your client information (perhaps in a portable plastic file box) and a secure area to store your client keys, should you choose to keep them on file.

If you have more room to spread out, then you can set up a full desk with a landline and desktop computer and a small filing cabinet. You still won't require much more space than just a 5-foot-by-5-foot area at most.

Whatever the size of your home office, you do have a definite advantage to utilizing a home office. The IRS gives you a home office deduction for your business. There are some strict guidelines you must adhere to in order to meet the requirements for the deduction, like setting aside that space as used only by your business.

Shhhh! I'm on the Phone!

Your biggest challenge in setting up your home office might lie in finding a quiet place to conduct professional phone conversations. You probably don't want to portray your business as one of a crying baby in the background or other noises that might be even more distracting to your clients. It's a good plan to have an area that you can set up with some privacy and noise barriers if possible. That might mean that your home office is set up in your bedroom or even a large walk-in closet if you don't have a spare bedroom and live with other people. Be sure that you let your family, friends, and other people know that when you are on a phone call with a new or current client, you require a businesslike atmosphere and are working.

When my kids were younger, we used a bandanna tied on my office door to signify that unless the "house was on fire" or some other serious event was taking place, I was not to be disturbed. That has worked well over the years. Now that my kids are older, I tell them, "I'm going to the office now to make some client phone calls. I'll let you know when I'm done." I still get the sneaky tiptoeing in and charades for what they might need on occasion, but for the most part, things run smoothly, and I can conduct phone calls with minimal interruptions and with the professional quality I want my clients to perceive. Just lay down the law with your family, and your phone conversations will run along as planned.

I don't meet with clients at my home, and I don't allow them to drop anything by my house. I do this to maintain my personal life separate from my business life. After your business grows, you don't want ten to fifteen people dropping by daily to give you their keys or payments. As much as possible you should try to focus your dealings with clients away from your residence.

In addition, you should rent a post office box to use for all of your business mailings. If your clients have your personal address, it allows them to stop by anytime they feel is appropriate. I've known several pet sitters who wished they'd never let their clients know where they live. Maintain a professional boundary between what is personal and what is business. Just because you have a home-based business doesn't mean that your home has to turn into pet-sitting central.

Hours of Operation—Pet-Sitting Visits and Phone Calls

You have two questions to think about for your hours of operation: What times will you offer visits, and what times will you be available to take and process new service bookings as they come in by phone or e-mail?

For your visits, keep in mind that people who are out of town and hire you for full-service vacation care will sometimes want early-morning and late-night visits. There are those clients we all like and want who have well-behaved dogs that are not on medication, have a doggy door, and who can be visited at 8 a.m. and 5 p.m., and everyone is happy. Nonmedicated cats are another easily accommodated client. But, unfortunately, they're not all that easy.

Our clients can schedule visits as early as 6:30 a.m. and as late as 9:30 p.m. We will not officially schedule anything before 6:30 a.m., and equally we will not

> My biggest pet peeve is poor phone preparation and pet-sitting businesses that don't understand the value of the phone in setting up a good impression and perception of their service and business. How you handle phone calls is as important as a great website and good customer service skills.

schedule anything later than 9:30 p.m. There are times when we get very busy, and our normal slots fill up. Then we have to shift those times to earlier for the a.m. and later for the p.m., but that is not our normal practice. These hours work well because a thirty-minute visit done at 9:30 p.m. means the sitter is leaving at 10 p.m. or a few minutes later. That gives the pet about eight and one-half hours until the first morning visit. You will need to establish set hours of your earliest and latest visits to what suits your schedule and your availability. You might not be able to offer care during the day for now if you are going to school or if you have another job, children at home, and other obligations. So take the time now to think about what your hours of availability and care will be. Write them down and do your best to stick to them. You can make exceptions if you must at any point in time, but don't let yourself get sucked into the trap of leaving your hours (especially mornings and late nights) open to whatever the client wants. You might find people asking (and they will) for visits at midnight and 3 a.m.

Your next decision to make is when you will take and return phone calls. Your phone can be your biggest asset or your worst enemy. Let's talk about phones first here for a minute.

Pet-sitting services that tout in their literature, website, and advertising that they provide professional service but answer the phone in a nonprofessional manner will be perceived in a nonprofessional light. This might seem like a small issue at first glance, but it is huge. Even though pet sitting has been around for about twenty years now and recognized by many people as a legitimate business, you will still find yourself battling people who don't understand the difference between your professional service and the kid down the street. Sometimes the first impression someone gets of your business is how you present your voice mail or how you answer your business phone line. Even if you can't afford a second line, set up your home phone or personal cell voice mail as your business. Tell friends and family to leave a message. Who knows? Maybe you'll catch a call from one of your friends whom you haven't had a chance to tell about your new venture, and she will hear your pet-sitting voice mail. You can tell her about your new career. It's easier to tell the people you know to just listen to your business message than it is to lose people looking for a professional service who hang up when they hear, "You've reached the home of John, Jane, Susie, and Joe and the office of Jane's Pet Sitting." Or, worse yet, "This is Jane. You know the routine." Trust me, an exclusive business voice mail, no matter how insignificant it seems to you, is worth it. In that same vein of reasoning, when you answer the phone associated with your business, you should always answer, "Good morning. Jane's Pet Sitting" or something that is a cheerful business greeting, not just "Hello." When you are starting your business, perception of who you are and your professional qualities will play as big a part as your personality and ability to gain the trust of your potential new clients.

I use a landline (with remote-access voice mail) as my main phone for business, but I know many pet sitters—probably the majority—who use their cell phone as their business phone. Both have pros and cons. Either way is fine, and landlines and cell phones are equally acceptable options.

Using a cell phone for your business line allows you a great business tool. On most phones now you can call, text, e-mail, and take photos of the pets in your care. However, keep in mind these guidelines:

- Do not answer calls while you are taking care of other people's pets. The people who hired you to care for their pets expect your 100 percent attention during your time at their home.
- Do not take calls of any nature while you are walking a dog. You might be too distracted to notice dangerous situations around you.
- Do not book clients from your cell phone if you are not in front of your scheduling planner. Dates that you think you will remember are easily forgotten, sticky notes in day planners get lost in car seats, and envelopes and slips of paper are easily lost.
- Do not talk to or text your clients while you are driving.

Let your voice mail do the work for you while you are actively pet sitting. Then address your phone messages in an orderly manner so everyone is safe and no dates are missed. This can be a training moment for your clients who might call and say, "I always get your voice mail." Explain to them that while you are actively out pet sitting or driving you do not take calls. When you explain to them why, you will gain their understanding and respect.

A huge hurdle that many pet sitters—even longtime pet sitters—face is after-hours calls. Although you want your clients to feel that they are the most important client to you anytime they call, there is a fine line you must walk in both your accessibility and in the emotional boundaries you set. Clients will call you with what they perceive as an emergency need. Establish office hours in which you will take and receive calls. You will want to set up a good voice mail system that has good sound quality and reliability so that your clients can leave messages anytime of the day and night. When you can't take a call or when the call comes after hours, let the voice mail take the message for you.

It's sometimes hard for your clients to understand that what they perceive as a booking emergency isn't necessarily so. What to them is a minute-by-minute emergency often isn't. Even with a sudden illness or death in the family, most bookings can wait until you open again in the morning. If clients learn of a situation requiring

Some after-hours calls involve medical issues that clients aren't sure how to handle. Because you are their trusted pet sitter, they are likely to call you when the veterinarian's office is closed, and the emergency pet clinic will not give them advice over the phone. You are the person they trust to know when something is wrong with their pet, likely you are certified in pet first aid and CPR, and probably you have the answers they might be seeking. Although having this trusted and professional relationship with your clients is important, you should remember that you are not a veterinarian and that you should not give medical advice to your clients. It is always safe to err on the side of caution by telling your clients to seek the advice of their veterinarian or the emergency pet care clinic in your area.

If the call comes after hours, and clients feel that their pet is ill or injured enough to see their regular veterinarian, they should be encouraged to go to the emergency clinic. You don't want to be responsible for giving the wrong advice. This can lead to a broken client relationship and even open you to litigation in some cases. Be compassionate, listen to the issue, and advise your clients that if you were in their shoes you would seek the advice of a veterinarian.

them to leave their home immediately, chances are that the first visit wouldn't have to happen for at least hours—at the soonest.

It is going to be up to you as the business owner to "train" your new and current clients on how you handle last-minute needs and animal medical emergencies. Fortunately, if you are consistent, these circumstances don't present themselves too often. If, however, you allow your clients to access you twenty-four hours a day, you will find that perceived emergencies pop up much more often.

Let your clients know that after they are signed up with your business, you are committed to helping them with their pet care. This fact is good to address at your initial meeting with the client and pet. Let them know how you handle calls and that should a last-minute emergency come up requiring them to leave town, they can count on you. Let them know that it's always good to book early for planned trips, but should an unforeseen emergency arise—an illness or a death in the family—they can call, even after hours, and leave you a message. Let them know that you would be happy to help them if ever this circumstance comes up and that you will call them as soon as you retrieve the message (but let them know it will likely be the next morning), and you will start care for their pets immediately. You will still get frantic phone calls about an unexpected trip that is last minute (and most often the more frantic people will call two, three, or four times and leave messages). But call your clients back when you get the message. When they say in relief, "Oh, thank goodness. I thought you wouldn't call," just calmly and sympathetically explain to them that you are happy to help but that generally your office closes at 4 p.m. The more consistent you are with sticking to some sort of office hours, the more compliant your clients will be, thus leaving you in the realm of sanity.

Of course, you, being the business owner, are going to set up your own office hours. If you "close" at 4 p.m., you need to be ready to check voice mail first thing in the morning (6:30 a.m. or earlier). If you don't think you will be up that early, close your phones later. Maybe calls after 8 p.m. will be returned the next day. Find something that feels right for your situation.

After you start pet sitting regularly, chances are that you might have some early-morning pet sitting. Checking the messages first thing in the morning when you get up and before you go to bed is a good practice. In that way, if any emergencies have popped up, you can handle them and literally "rest easy" and sleep well at night. Here's the nitty gritty of it. You need to be in control of your business enough to allow you to completely focus on the pet sitting you do each day, so setting limits on

> Your office voice mail might sound something like this: "Thank you for calling Cathy's Critter Care. We aren't available to take your call now—we are probably out caring for our furry friends—but we will get back to you at our earliest convenience. As a reminder, our office hours are Monday through Saturday 10 a.m. to 4 p.m. We will address after-hours emergencies at the earliest possible time. If you need information, check out our website at www.MyPetsitterOnline.com."

your phone call return policy is perfectly acceptable. Most days I check my voice mail once in the morning, once in the evening, and once just before bedtime. I answer calls as they come in if possible. If not possible, and I know I have messages waiting for me, I check them and address them right away. Before I hired my office assistant, I actually kept fairly short hours when people could get me on the phone simply because I was out pet sitting. You will be, too! Reinforce to your clients that they are welcome to leave a message for you and that you will return their call.

Last-Minute Lucys

There are people who don't plan for their pet care. You might get after-hours calls from potential new clients who need care right away. If you are able to help these people, that's great. If not, don't sweat it too much because these folks tend to be your problem clients in many other areas over the course of your care with them. Many of these "last-minute Lucys" call at 10 o'clock at night for pet sitting starting the next day. When you call them back the next day either they've found someone else to do it, or they're already out of town. Don't beat yourself up about missing a potential new client. You will be saving your sanity by not being a slave to your phone.

Your Client Files—Paper and Electronic

I am a strong proponent of using one of the scheduling software systems written for the pet-sitting profession. They keep you organized, allow you to e-mail clients, process credit cards efficiently, and store your client data in a retrievable format. Whether you choose a computer hard drive–based system like that of Petrax (www .petraxsoftware.com), an Internet-based solution like Bluewave Professional Pet Sitter (www.professionalpetsitter.com), or Power Pet Sitter (www.powerpetsitter .com), all of the systems have a good base for storing the important information you retrieve from your clients at your initial meeting and as you work for them over several years. You can easily update the information on pet feeding, alarm codes, and additions of pets to the family. After you build your business up to a client base of fifty or more, you will benefit from the use of these software programs for booking your clients and keeping their information current.

However, do not discount the importance of having a hard copy file for each of your clients. Not only do you need a signed consent agreement for legal purposes, but also you want to have some backup for basic client information should your computer crash or the Internet connection go down when you need information.

You should set up a plan to have both electronic and paper copies of all of your clients. As mentioned earlier, a portable file box or a small, locking filing cabinet are good options to store your client files. Keep your client informational service agreement (see pages 174 and 175) along with any other paperwork, notes, or any other information for each client in a file folder labeled with client's last name and first name and alphabetized by last name. On the tab of each folder, you can also write the date of your initial meeting with the client. This is a good date to use to track how long a client has been with you and to acknowledge his anniversary date with your business each year.

> You shouldn't take any bookings when you are not looking at your calendar and able to write the dates on it immediately.

Remember that your electronic and paper client information is highly sensitive data and should be treated as such. If you use a portable file box, it should be stored in a locking safe so that it's not easily carried off by someone other than you. Your filing cabinet should lock if you choose to use that for storage.

You should maintain one calendar that has all of your pet-sitting assignments listed on it. Even if you are using a good software program, as a backup a calendar can be a lifesaver. Whether you use a wall calendar or notebook or planner mobile calendar will be up to you. They are both good options.

Handling Your Clients' Keys

Along with your client information in electronic and paper form, your clients' keys are items you should treat with extreme caution. Chapter 5 details handling your clients'

You will need a computer of some sort to effectively manage your business if you want to generate at least a part-time income. Websites and e-mail have become such a huge part of our daily life that you will be missing out on a huge client base if you don't invest in a computer. You don't need all the bells and whistles in a computer. Just something to adequately access the Internet, do some basic word processing, and, if you are using a hard drive–based software booking system, run the program.

keys and the many options you have for doing so. It's not recommended that you store clients' keys with client information because those two in combination in the wrong hands can lead to a breach in your clients' homes. The good news is that your clients' keys will not take up a large portion of your office. More on keys in detail in Chapter 5.

Your Mobile Office

Due to the nature of pet sitting, after your business gets going, you will be spending a lot of time in your car. Therefore, you will also have your mobile office. If you are using a cell phone or smart phone, then a big portion of your office is already with you. Remember, though, that when you are outside your home office, your focus is on safely arriving at each client's home and caring for her pets and property. If you have to take a call or look up information on your smart phone, pull over to the side of the road.

You will need an arsenal of tools of the trade with you in your car/mobile office: leashes, plastic poop bags, extra cat scoop, pet toys, thank you cards for clients, business cards, business pens, and notepads (I call them "visitation logs") that you leave for your client with notes from your visits.

I've found that a plastic storage tote or bin that you can get at any popular discount store works well to keep your mobile office supplies together and in good shape in your car.

The Least You Need to Know
- You don't need much room to set up a home-based pet-sitting office. A space as small as a corner table and a laptop with a secure locking safe are all you need.

- You will set up a mobile office in your vehicle as well as your home office.
- You will face challenges maintaining your personal life and your business life. Think about how you will separate the two so that your clients don't have full access to you twenty-four/seven.
- There are software systems written specifically for the professional pet sitter.

Action Steps

- Find your home office space.
- Determine what kind of phone you will use for your business (cell/smart phone or landline). If you will need to buy a phone, how much will it cost?
- Do you have a computer and Internet connection? If not, determine how you will use the convenience of e-mail for your business. You might consider the library until you can buy a computer.
- Rent a post office box for your business.

Getting Started

A business plan is a road map for your business. When completed, the business plan will outline the major aspects of your home-based pet-sitting business. Most home-based pet-sitting businesses can be started with little additional financing needed. However, if you decide that you need additional funding to start your business, a business plan will be required by your lenders.

Writing a business plan can be a daunting task, but don't let it scare you into not doing it. Don't let your eagerness to start walking dogs and scooping cat boxes outweigh the importance of writing your business plan. It's a key tool in getting your business off to the right start.

Really, a business plan is a basic map for where your business will start, where it will go, and even how it might end. You wouldn't plan a cross-country road trip without some sort of idea or map of where you are going and when you might be leaving or returning. Planning makes your travel easier. Even if you are traveling with an open agenda, a map and plan of where you are going are the most basic of tools. They help you decide what might be good decisions for your trip and what might not work. Your business plan will compel you to look at the business strengths and weaknesses and prepare for challenges as best you can before you leash up your first pup.

Numerous books are devoted to writing a business plan. If you encounter problems writing your plan, you

Don't skip this chapter! Even if you don't want to write your business plan just yet, this chapter is full of pointers on thinking through pricing, services, and marketing.

should be able to check out a good business plan book at your local library. However, we've devoted a lot of time and detail here because if anything is going to get missed as the average pet sitter opens her business, it will be the business plan. That shouldn't be the case. At the end of working through this chapter you will be able to draw up a well-thought-out plan of action for your business.

The biggest challenge in writing a business plan is knowing how the business will operate when it's not even open yet. How do you know what revenues you can produce? How could you begin to even know? It's okay to make educated guesses based on your research into your market and competition. Business plans are dynamic documents. They can be modified based on updated information as often as necessary. You aren't stuck with doing things a certain way because that's what it says in your plan. The business plan simply gives the concept of your home-based pet-sitting business some boundaries, guidelines, and structure. When I started Cathy's Critter Care, I envisioned only a business with enough clients to support a part-time income for me. Over the course of the life of my business, I've had to

As the SBA website reads, "If you don't plan for the success of your business, you will likely fail."

A business plan:

- Is required for financing from a lender

- Is necessary as a road map for your business

- Should be revisited/revised at least once per year

Confused by what a business plan should look like? Just get on the Internet and do some simple searches for "business plan templates" or "business plan example." There are even some good worksheets online at www.score.org. Just don't let yourself get bogged down by the overwhelming plans out there. Every business plan has its basic structure. A simple and good business plan is all you need to be successful. There are no requirements on length, and honestly, sometimes the shorter the business plan, the better it reads. Don't try to pad your plan with extra information that isn't really needed to show what your business will do, who will do it, how it will be done, and how it will be profitable. That's all a business plan needs to have to be a good one.

modify my business plan many times to encompass where it is today. We now employ on average fifteen part-time pet sitters and one full-time office assistant. It can't be said enough that your business plan is something that needs to be revisited regularly. Just as you shouldn't proceed with your pet-sitting business without a plan, you also shouldn't write your plan, set it on a shelf, and never look at it again. Keep that idea of a road map in mind. Sometimes travel plans are modified due to circumstances either within or beyond our control. So, too, goes the business plan. You might find it challenging to find enough time to revisit your plan. After all, our goal is to be busy working so we can sustain our business. Make it a priority to look at your business plan and update it at least once per year. After you have it written, it should be easy to modify within a reasonable amount of time.

Basic Elements of a Business Plan

A comprehensive plan will include the following elements:

- Executive summary
- Market analysis
- Company/business description and vision
- Organization and management
- Marketing and sales
- Description of services
- Funding
- Financials
- Appendix

The Cover Sheet

You can't judge a book by its cover, but it sure can pique the interest of the reader. Start with a neat, clean, four-color cover page for your business plan. Your cover sheet will have the name of your business, logo, your business address, phone number, and website. This will help put the business plan, should it need to be presented to anyone else, in perspective of what it is and who it belongs to. This is especially important if you present the document to any investors for additional funding.

Title Page

Include a title page to give some outline of your business plan and to allow readers to easily find the information they are looking for.

Section 1: The Executive Summary

The executive summary will be the first section of your business plan but will be the last section you write. It will be easier to write after you've compiled all the other sections and information. It will be a concise (approximately one to two pages) yet detailed summary of your business to include:

- Owners—experience and background
- Mission statement
- Location of business
- Number of employees
- Description of services
- Location of business
- Future plans for business

Start right now by jotting down a few sentences under each of the preceding categories. After you have just one or two sentences for each category and your mission statement, set aside this portion of your business plan and move on to the market analysis. We will revisit the executive summary at the end of this chapter and fill in the holes.

When you write your executive summary be sure to include what decisions led you to the idea of opening your home-based pet-sitting business and how you can satisfy the needs of your target market of clients. Because there will likely be competition already established in the area, highlight how you plan to do a better job and what skills you bring to your work that will make you a better choice for pet care. Perhaps better availability is the key to your success. Or you will provide specialized care or overnight service. Whatever ideas you believe will drive clients to call you, focus on those ideas in your executive summary.

The SBA (www.sba.gov) offers online workshops for writing your first business plan. It's easy to sign up. A one-page registration is all that is required. It's free and takes thirty minutes to complete. The information is invaluable. If you have a computer, log on and take the course.

Mission Statement

Now is the time to write your mission statement. Don't worry: It's easy and uncomplicated. A mission statement is different from a tag line or motto. It can be as short as a few words to as long as a couple of sentences. When you write your mission statement, try to keep your scope broad while giving a concise idea of the services you will provide.

Focus on the who, what, and why of your business. The "who," of course, is you, but maybe you envision having staff in the future, so using the business name in the mission statement is usually a better idea than using "I" or "we." The "what" is what you will be doing: providing pet sitting, pet care, full-service pet sitting. These are all appropriate terms and phrases. The "why" of the business is where you can be creative and inspirational. A good starting point for your mission statement is your business name and the word *will*. Avoid words like *try, strive,* and *attempt*. Choose strong action words like *will, accomplish, complete,* and *fulfill*.

There is a world of difference between these two mission statements:

- TLC will provide pet-sitting services to the people living in Orange County.
- TLC will offer premium in-home pet care with affordable pricing and superior, reliable, and trustworthy pet sitters offering a variety of services and support to pet clients and their people.

You want your mission statement to accurately portray your service but also to highlight what makes your business a good choice. Now is the time to toot your own horn. Write several mission statement samples with different word choices that you can look at. Put them on separate sheets of paper so you can move back and forth between them. Write out five to six potential mission statements using different structures, words, and thoughts. Review them and pick what you like from each. Ask yourself, "What kind of impression does this mission statement give?" After you've selected your favorite two or three possible mission statements, let trusted friends look at them and give you feedback on what they like and don't like about each one

> Cathy's Critter Care will provide reliable, conscientious, complete, and skilled in-home pet sitting for our pet clients and total peace of mind for their owners through a team of pet-care experts providing professional service and personal care.

and which one is their favorite. Ask them to view your mission statement as a client would with fresh eyes.

Do a quick Internet search of "pet sitting mission statement" to get an idea of what other people have used. Here's an example of some mission statements:

- ABC pet sitting will provide personal pet care to our clients and their people with caring, honest, and dependable service, allowing pets to stay in the comfort of their home.
- XYZ pet sitting will focus on in-home care for pets, giving their people total peace of mind when they have to be away.
- ABC pet sitting will fulfill the pet-care needs of our clients through honest, reliable, and loving in-home pet sitting and a full scope of additional pet services.

From Mission to Vision

Now let's look at what the future might hold for your business and write a vision statement, too. The vision statement will outline what the future holds for the company and should guide the company and mission statement. Think about what your business might be or do three or five years down the road. Will you be the primary source for clients to turn to for all of their pet-sitting needs? Will you have staff driving ABC Pet Sitting vehicles from house to house? Will you expand into kenneling or even provide innovative ways for your customers to travel with their pets? Think about the big picture in an altruistic, enlightening, and inspirational way. What is your ultimate goal for your business both financially and even ethically?

You can get a good idea of some examples of vision statements by taking a look online. There are plenty out there to look at to get a good start. Just keep in mind that a vision statement, like a mission statement, can, and should, be reviewed, revisited, and revised annually to ensure it still meets the scope of where your business is headed. If you are having problems getting your vision statement out, you might want to flesh out some more of the details of your business through your business plan and then come back and insert your vision statement.

To give you a good idea of a well-written business plan, www.bplans.com has several free examples.

Section 2: The Market Analysis

The market analysis will describe the state of the pet-sitting industry and your position. Start by doing some quick research on the overall state of the pet-sitting industry. You can get some great information at either of the two national organizations:

- Pet Sitters International (www.petsit.org)
- National Association of Professional Pet Sitters (www.petsitters.org)

Write an overview of the current state of pet sitting. Is it growing, stable, or declining in the number of businesses? Why is this a good home-based business to go into? Feel free to glean some of your information from this book. Remember that the pet industry is considered to be one of the strongest industries and is said to be recession proof. Even if people stop traveling for leisure, you can focus more of your marketing and advertising on business travelers and their pets. Think about these kinds of angles as you write your market analysis and point out ways in which your pet-sitting business will draw on the strengths of the pet-care industry, but be able to redirect your plans in case one aspect of your business dries up. You have to establish the viability of the industry so that it makes sense to go into business. For example, video rental brick-and-mortar stores have gone by the wayside with the advent of online rental and even downloads. Luckily, the pet-sitting industry is growing as more people want the convenience, safety, and security of leaving their pets at home with a professional.

Next outline the businesses that are already in the market and are providing services similar to yours. This is where your research in Chapter 2 comes in. You can even include a table like the one you prepared in Chapter 2 to easily outline what competition you have. Then hit on the major points of how you will do a better job of serving clients in your target market than those businesses you've listed as your competition. Will you provide services they don't? Will you provide online booking or twenty-four-hour access to you through an answering service or longer visits or free gifts with bookings? Brainstorm ways in which any pet-sitting business, not necessarily yours, could provide added benefits to its clients and outdo the competition. Doing this will get you to thinking about the ways in which you can do a better job than your competition in meeting clients' needs. In addition, don't forget the importance of highlighting networking opportunities with other pet sitters and pet professionals like veterinarians, groomers, and doggy day cares. If there are networking meetings you will attend, be sure to include that in your market analysis.

Your Target Market

Your target market is the group of potential clients to which you will be able to provide services. This market will include a geographical area and a description of the people or households in that geographical area for whom you can work. For example, a target market statement for ABC Cat Care might be: "ABC Cat Care will provide pet sitting to cat owners living in the zip code 78154 who desire in-home care for their pets at least once per day and have an income such that they can afford to hire a professional pet-sitting service." Be honest about what your target market is. It does your business no good to say you will care for all of the cats in your geographical area. Although you might be willing to do that, you need to narrow your target market to those people who will be able to use your services. If your business will include most of the options available for pet sitting as well as house sitting, your target market statement might read something like this: "XYZ Total Home and Pet Care will provide home checks and pet sitting for clients with a household income of $60,000 or more living in a 15-mile radius of Pond Creek, Texas, who own dogs, cats, small caged animals, birds, reptiles, or livestock." Potential clients of XYZ who do not have pets can utilize home checks and house-sitting services. Keep in mind that this is simply your target market. This doesn't mean that you cannot help someone outside that target market if your phone rings and you can provide the service the caller needs. However, a well-defined target market leads to a well-developed and less-costly advertising campaign later (more on that in "Marketing"). You will want to focus your money on getting jobs from the people who need you and can afford your care. You might want to include in your target market assessment how that market might grow in the future. Is the geographical area in a growth phase of new homes (and thus new pet owners moving to the area)? Is a large company looking to move into the area (and provide you with potential midday dog-walking clients)?

Your target market is:

- Where you will provide service (geographical location)
- What kind of service you will provide (cat only, midday dog walking, house sitting)
- Who will use your service (need + income)

After you have established the viability of the industry as a whole and your ability to draw clients to your business, your market analysis is complete. Pretty simple!

Sample company description:

CCC provides in-home pet sitting to clients residing in the Schertz, Texas, community. CCC will travel to the clients' home, take care of all the pets' needs, as well as basic home care, like bringing in the mail and watering plants. CCC will be managed from a home-based office, and all visits will be conducted by Cathy Vaughan. CCC will be operated as a sole proprietorship.

Section 3: The Company/Business Description

Your company description will convey what your business is. Essentially it is what you are going to tell people when they ask the question, "What do you do?" You are going to be providing pet-sitting services with a home-based office. Will you be the only person working in the business, or will you have a partner or employee, or will your spouse or other family member help you?

The Full Picture

Now let's describe how you will conduct your business. Some points to address in your company description section are:

- Membership in a national pet-sitting organization—will you be a member of one, both, or neither?
- Who will provide your business liability insurance?
- Who will provide your bond policy if necessary?
- Will you have any suppliers such as online booking software?
- What mode of transportation will you use to travel from house to house?
- Where will you get your printing done? Will you be paperless?
- Will you leave gifts for your clients or provide them with goods? If so, which supplier(s) will you use?
- How will your clients book your service—through phone (cell or landline or both), Internet/e-mail? What Internet service provider will you use?
- Will you have a website? If so, how will that, and potentially other social media, tie in to your business, and how will it operate and drive new clients to you or keep current clients loyal?

Goal!

An important part of your business description is setting specific and attainable goals and outlining clear objectives. The reason you want to go into business for yourself is to make the decisions that impact your life. Take some time to think about the things that are important for you. Are you looking to make enough money to quit your full-time job? Do you want more time with your family or more leisure time? Are you looking at a pet-sitting business as a way to build a wealthy venture in which you will hire staff sitters and possibly franchise? What is your vision for your business at the beginning, a year from now, three years from now, and even longer down the road? Be prepared to address how you will meet these goals as well. Will you provide as easier booking process for clients so that you can accommodate people looking for a streamlined process? Will you work in conjunction with your local humane society to provide pet sitting at a discount for any adopted pets? Perhaps you might even want to set up your home-based pet-sitting business such that you are the office manager, and you hire pet sitters to complete the visits. Go back to your vision for your business and brainstorm what those heartfelt goals are.

"A goal properly set is halfway reached."

—*Abraham Lincoln*

Some goals might be:

- To launch a home-based pet-sitting business with startup costs of less than $500
- To remain a single-sitter service without hiring support through staff and maintain one-on-one customer care
- To build a client base to support a part-time income within one year
- To provide the community of pet owners with an available option for professional pet sitting
- To establish the business as a leader in the pet-sitting field within three years and mentor new people looking to start a pet-sitting business
- To establish a network of pet-sitting professional businesses that will refer business to each other, thus helping all involved
- To reach monthly gross sales of $5,000 by the end of four years in business
- To employ and manage five part-time pet sitters within three years
- To replace a full-time income within five years of the start of the business

You will set your own goals. Perhaps none of the preceding goals interests you and how you envision your business. Think about what is important to you. Maybe replacing a part-time income is what you are looking for to provide flexibility in your schedule, allowing you to spend more time with your family. Perhaps you would like your spouse to work with you, so setting a goal of replacing a full-time income is important to you. Think about why you want to start your own business aside from the fact that you love animals and want to care for them. If that was your only reason, you could volunteer your time at a shelter or rescue group. Most people want to start their own business so that they are in charge of what happens to them. They make the decisions and are responsible for their destiny. In your goals put down what you want that destiny to be.

Your goals need to be specific and attainable. I have to tell you, though, that when I started Cathy's Critter Care in 1998, I never, in a million years, would have believed that what we do now was even possible. We've replaced two full-time incomes at this point. That's why it is important to review, revisit, and revise your business plan periodically. Write down what you really want.

Section 4: Description of Services

In this section you will identify those services that you will provide and prices for each item and how they will be competitive with other businesses providing pet-sitting services in the area.

Your list might contain services such as pet washing, nail clipping, and even behavior training. Be sure to price your services when booked in conjunction with your primary business of pet sitting and when booked alone if they will be offered. You will want to pull out each item and address specifically what each item covers.

Pet-sitting standard visit—thirty minutes: Full pet care for all pets in the home is provided at the client's home. Ancillary services provided will be picking up mail, watering plants, attending to garbage.

Extended visit—forty-five minutes: All services of standard visit are provided with additional time allotted for pet visit/walks, etc.

Pet taxi—safe, comfortable transportation for pets from one location to another

Pet-Sitting Visits

Standard—thirty minutes = $19

Extended—forty-five minutes = $26

Express add-on—fifteen minutes = $14

Medication required = $3 per pet per administration

Overnight care 8 p.m.–6 a.m. = $75

Pet taxi service = $15 pickup fee + $0.75 per mile from pickup to dropoff

Pooper scooping in conjunction with pet sitting = additional $15 added to first visit, yard maintained throughout services without additional fees

Pooper scooping only (no pet-sitting services booked) = $20 for one pet, one service scheduled or once a month scheduled. One pet service scheduled and paid for weekly $16, biweekly $18.

Address how you will be competitive as the market stands presently. Are your prices lower than those of others or higher but with added value? How do your services compare with those of others? If what you are offering is the same as what others are offering, and the prices are the same, what will drive clients to you?

In your market analysis have you discovered a need for more pet sitters in the area? This might be the case, so why reinvent the wheel? What is out there is working for the businesses. They are successful, and the prices are in line with the perceived value to clients. The fact that you have availability, are accessible, and are great at customer service and communication will draw clients to you. If you've established a relationship with other pet-sitting businesses, mention these connections in your competitive edge as a way that you will gain clients.

How will your business be able to draw new customers in, meet their needs, and change as necessary?

Section 5: Organization and Management

What is the legal structure of your business?

- Sole proprietor
- Partnership
- LLC (limited liability company)
- Corporation (S Corp or C Corp)

Who will work in your business? Who are the key players? Perhaps it's just you or maybe you and a partner or even a group of people who established the business. Whatever your scenario, describe the people who will work in the business and what their backgrounds are. What other jobs have they held? What special skills do they/ you bring to the business?

If more than one person will work in the business, describe how the job duties will be split up and delegated. Who will do what?

What licenses or permits do you need to operate your pet-sitting business? Pet sitting is unregulated, so you generally do not need a license. However, you might consider becoming certified through an online course or obtain pet first aid certification. If these items are in your plans, address them here. Will you obtain your additional training prior to beginning actual pet-sitting visits? If not, then when will you obtain this additional training?

An S-corporation is one in which, for tax purposes, the income of the business is passed through the business without being taxed. The members of the S-corporation report profits or losses from the business on their personal tax returns. This is known as single taxation or pass through taxation. The money passes through the S-corporation without being taxed. There are some limitations on the types of small businesses that can be structured as an S-corporation, but most pet-sitting companies meet all of the requirements. Visit www.IRS.gov for more information on the requirements.

A C-corporation is structured such that the company's profits are taxed, as well as the dividends that are distributed to the company's members or shareholders. It is rare for a pet-sitting company to be structured as a C-corporation.

Every business should be registered in its county and in some instances and locales, city or state registration may be required for both accountability purposes and taxation. Be sure to check with your city, county, and state business licensing offices to determine if this is required for your area.

List in this section your insurance information and membership in any organizations you plan to join.

Section 6: Marketing and Sales Strategy

You're ready and willing to pet sit. How will you attract new customers? How will you let everyone know you are open and are the best option for pet care? Marketing is the process of creating new customers.

In this section you want to address these important questions. Will your previous boss, a veterinarian, be referring business to you? Will you set up booths at local pet events, distribute free doggy bandannas at a pet walk or a school, wrap your car in advertising, set up a website? Keep in mind there are four p's in marketing. Becoming a viable business means positioning yourself in an optimal way in at least one of these areas. Address in your marketing and sales strategy plan how your pricing, promotion, products (services), or place (location) will bring you a sufficient market share of clients to meet your goals as outlined.

> It is not the strongest of the species that survives, nor the most intelligent, but rather the one most responsive to change.
>
> —Author Unknown

This is a good time to address what will happen if the market shifts and some, or a majority, of your market shrinks. Be prepared to explain how your business will adjust to changes in the market by either growing or being able to contract if needed or even continue down a different path if the market warrants.

The Four P's of Marketing
Price
Promotion
Products (services)
Place

Address how your business will use the four p's of marketing to establish itself in the market successfully. Will your price be significantly lower than the competition's, driving new clients to you? Will you send out direct mailers, put out door hangers, attend all of the area animal events, and be a member of various social groups revolving around pets, thus utilizing promotion to position your business in the market? Will your services be different in such a manner that you can draw in a client niche not previously served? Are you one of only a few pet sitters in your area so that your "place" is the driving force in your marketing plan?

Section 7: Financial Management

This section will explain how your business will make money. After all, that's why we are opening a business. We hope to make money. The financial management section will need to include financial statements for the business and predictions on the future money-making capability of the business by estimating revenues through the first three years of the business. The financial management section should show how much money (or other assets) the business has now, how much money is planned for expenses after the business is operating, and how much money the business plans to make as a net profit at any given point in time.

Three Documents Required for Financial Management Section

- Balance sheet
- Income statement
- Cash flow statement

If you have a good friend in accounting, and you are feeling a little shaky in this area, ask that friend for help in building these documents for you.

You need to supply three financial documents in this section. Wait! Don't close the book and run for the hills. Most people who are great pet sitters and want to

NOTE: These documents do not have anything to do with IRS filings, although having a good income statement monthly will help you compile your taxes quarterly or annually.

All three of your financial documents are dependent on some key information about your business: income or revenue, assets, expenses.

open their own pet-sitting business are terrified of the *a*-word: *accounting*. The good news is that because you are starting a new business, the forms will be easy to complete. Start now. Go ahead: Dive in and do your best. Do some studying and make sure you have a good grasp of what each document is meant to convey about your business and how it is used. If you get a good handle on these documents now, it will be easier down the road to compile them and provide them to anyone wanting to see your financial records when you are making money and want to expand.

The Balance Sheet

The balance sheet shows the assets the business currently has in comparison with its liabilities. The balance sheet shows what is called the "net worth" of a business. It doesn't necessarily show how much gross or net revenue a business makes over any given time. The balance sheet simply focuses on what is owned or due to the business in accounts receivable and what is owed by the business.

Assets might be money in the bank, cash on hand, or anything already purchased for the business like tangible items such as desks, supplies, or a computer. Assets might also include prepaid services like insurance or membership in a national organization or local chamber of commerce. Basically, assets include anything the business owns at the present time (and the date of the balance sheet) or has paid for already and will be using in the course of business.

The opposite of assets is liability. A liability is anything the business currently owes for. On your balance sheet you will not include items that are due annually that you haven't paid for and are not currently due. For example, if you anticipate purchasing some kind of Internet-based booking system that charges monthly, you would include only one-month's charge on your balance sheet as a liability and not the entire year's charge.

The balance sheet is often said to be a "snapshot in time." That means that the value on the balance sheet is the value of that business for that particular date in time. The value might have been different just one day prior to that date or one day after. But the balance sheet must accurately reflect where the business stands at that given time.

Chances are that if you are starting your business from scratch, you might not have very many accounts receivable (people who owe you money) or even accounts payable (people to whom you owe money). You might have some cash on hand set aside for the business and some other assets, so be sure to include those. Include

> The balance sheet, unlike its name, doesn't have to "balance." It simply shows the assets and liabilities of a business and the net worth at one point in time.

anything you've purchased for the business, too, like this book. Your balance sheet might be very simple right now. That's okay. It just needs to be accurate.

The Income Statement

The income statement is set up in two sections: revenue and expenses. Sometimes an income statement is called a "profit and loss statement" because at the end of the page, you will be able to determine if your business saw a profit or a loss in revenue during the specified time your income statement covers.

If you are starting your pet-sitting business from scratch at the reading of this book, then your income statement for your business plan will be a projection-based document. You will need to predict what you will earn in a given period of time and what you will spend. Doing this will take some research on your part into the market in which you are conducting your business. It will be a good idea to work out three separate income statements for your first three years in business, especially if you are seeking financing from an outside source. By preparing three separate income statements, you can accurately portray the beginning of your business and show growth, especially in years 2 and 3. Remember that an income statement will show income for a specific period of time. You pick the time frame for any income statement you write.

Writing an income statement might seem like a huge task right now, and after all, we want to get out and rub some bellies. That's more fun, of course. But roll up your sleeves because getting your financials in order now will help you better navigate through your first year in business, see where you are spending money, and see how much money you are making. The income statements you prepare for your business plan won't be the last ones you sit down to complete. To keep track of your business finances,

> For a startup pet-sitting business, it is good to show income for the first three years in business as separate statements for year 1, year 2, and year 3.

you should complete an income statement either biannually or annually. Getting comfortable with the terms, methods of preparation, and categories on an income statement now will serve you well in your first few years in business.

The income statement has only two sections. Let's take a look at each section and work our way through them both.

Revenue

First let's estimate your total revenue or gross sales (that's line item 1 on the sample income statement, see page 77). How many visits will you complete in a day during your first month of business? Maybe zero. That's okay. It takes time to get established and get the word out. How many visits do you anticipate completing in your second month of business? Again, it is safe to say that perhaps you won't have seen a single paying client during this time. Does that mean you won't be working? No, of course not. You will be using your first several months in business to market, advertise, and quite possibly provide some free pet-sitting services to people to establish references and start word-of-mouth advertising.

If you've already been doing some pet sitting for friends, neighbors, and coworkers as a hobby or a favor, then you probably have a good idea of how many paid assignments you will complete in any given time. If this is the case, then you can certainly set an estimate that accurately reflects the number of visits you will be paid for.

Let's say that by the end of six months in business, with sufficient marketing, advertising, and promoting of your new pet-sitting business, you will be completing, on average, two visits per day, or about sixty visits per month. Not bad. So how does that translate into gross sales for the year? Don't worry about how many of each type of visit (if you set different price points for different types of care) you will be completing at this point. This is just an estimate of your total gross revenue, so using an average price is fine. Later in the life of your businesses, you might want to pull out different categories under your gross sales, such as thirty-minute visits, forty-five-minute visits, pet taxi service, and overnight care. Doing this will help you track within your gross sales any changes within that category. But for now we will estimate just on your average visit.

Complete the following table for your first twelve months in business with estimates of the number of visits you will complete monthly. Keep in mind the cyclical nature of the pet-sitting business as you estimate how many visits you will complete.

Estimate how much your business will grow monthly as well. Is your goal to increase your client base by 5 percent monthly? Then use that number to translate the growth in your higher-revenue months into the number of visits you will be completing.

Your first income statement for the initial year in business will need to show your forecast for the total gross sales for that time frame. So, if you think you will start completing, on average, sixty visits per month starting in your third month of business and continuing through your twelfth month, you will have completed six hundred visits total in the first year of business (sixty visits a month for ten months). Now multiply this total by your average price per visit, and you have your total gross sales. Fill that in on the first line of your income statement. Be sure to use the numbers that you believe will accurately reflect your business.

Month	Number of Estimated Visits	Total Gross Sales

Higher-Volume Months for Pet Sitting	Lower-Volume Months for Pet Sitting
March	January
May	February
June	April
July	September
August	October
November	
December	

Calculating Gross Sales

visits x average price per visit = gross sales

60 visits x $17 = $1,020

Keep in mind the time of year you are starting your business. If you open in October, you might see a big jump in business in your second month (Thanksgiving) and third month (Christmas). Write your income statement for the first year in business to accurately reflect what will happen with your business during that time frame and be able to support your theories and estimates with your research.

The second item you need to address in the revenue section is sales returns and allowances. Technically anytime you make a sale, that amount goes into your gross sales category. If you need to refund part or all of a client's fees paid, then it will need to go here. If you do a good job, show up at a client's home as requested, and fulfill the client's needs, your returns and allowances will be zero. By the time you finish reading this book, you will have a good set of standards to follow, and your returns and allowances should be very low. For projection purposes on your income statements for your business plan, it is safe to leave returns and allowances at zero. Remember that this category is important for your overall monthly accounting.

Expenses

Some of the variable expenses for a new home-based pet-sitting business are:

Advertising

Bad debts (money owed to you that is past due)

Bank charges

Contract labor

Credit card fees

Delivery expenses

Office supplies

Postage

Professional fees (could be anything from legal to grooming)

Payroll taxes

Vehicle expenses (including mileage)

In the expenses section of your income statement, you will list all the ways your business spent money for the time frame listed on your income statement (see page 77). The categories listed in the sample income statement are also the major categories you

As your income goes up, generally your variable expenses will go up, too, because they are tied to the amount of work you are doing.

- To estimate your vehicle expenses, you can use one of two methods approved by the IRS.
- Save all of your receipts for maintenance and repairs and your gas receipts.
- Keep track of your mileage for any business travel (visits or post office and supply runs) and take the standard per-mile deduction the IRS allows.

will see on your end-of-the-year tax forms. So keeping an accurate account of these expenses not only will give you a true picture of the money you are spending and the money you are making by looking at your bottom-line figures but will also simplify your end-of-year tax tasks. You will need to specify how much you will spend on fixed expenses like Internet and telephone service and membership dues. You will also need to predict what you will spend on expenses that might vary like postage, supplies, and vehicle expenses like gas.

Sometimes it is hard to predict varying expenses, but remember that as your income goes up, generally your varying expenses will go up, too, because they are tied to the amount of work you are doing. For example, how do you estimate vehicle (gas) expenses?

Remember to prepare three income statements. The first will show your business specifics for the first six months, the second for the first full year, and the third for the second full year in business. How much would you like for your business to grow in each of those time frames? A 10–20 percent increase in visit volume and revenue from your first year in business to your second year in business will be considered appropriate and is attainable if you continue to market aggressively.

Use the numbers from your first income statement to extrapolate logically your second six months in business.

Pet sitting is cyclical in nature. Keep this fact in mind when you are working on your projections. Your annual projections will even out the highs and lows, but if you work out any monthly figures (for example, your first six months in business), remember to allow for slow times in January, February, September, and October.

Cash Flow Statement

The last financial document you will need for your business plan is the cash flow statement. This document reflects your actual cash on hand at any given time (or your projection-based cash on hand if your business plan is projection based). The cash flow statement is a snapshot of liquid assets (cash on hand) at a given point in time, and more importantly it shows how money flows through the business. The cash flow statement gives an account of the money coming in based on your projections minus the expenses incurred at that point in time and shows a final bottom line of a positive cash amount on hand or a deficit. A key difference between the cash flow statement and the income statement is that the cash flow statement doesn't take into account future cash coming into the business by means of credit. It simply shows for any given time period what came in to the business and what the money was spent on.

Your cash flow statement can be the simplest of your three financial documents and the most easily understood. Simply start with your investment money, if any, as your starting funds, and estimate your sales for the given time frame (six months, year 1, and year 2). This will be your total income. Total your estimated expenses for the time frame and subtract them from the income. This is a simple cash flow statement. If you have any business investments or pay any interest on loans, these will need to be added in, but generally speaking the startup home-based pet-sitting business needs only a simple format to show that the money coming in to the business will support the expenses and leave a profit.

Appendix

The appendix portion of your business plan will include any supporting documents that show your plan for a pet-sitting business to be viable. You can include items like surveys that you present to potential clients, research from newspapers and magazine articles, as well as any market or demographic research that supports the viability of your business.

You can include reference letters from potential customers and from pet-industry colleagues like veterinarians and dog trainers. If you design any advertising materials like your logo, brochures, and business cards, include them in your appendix. You can include any business forms like your service agreements, policies, and any other booking forms you use.

Returning to the Executive Summary

Now that you've worked your way through the entire business plan, you have a solid idea of what your business will do, to whom you will provide services, and how you will run the day-to-day operations. It's time to revisit the executive summary portion of your plan and flesh out the details of each section with the work you've already completed in compiling the rest of your business plan.

Now the challenge will be to include the following information in just one page:

- Owners—experience and background
- Mission statement
- Location of business
- Number of employees
- Description of services
- Location of business
- Future plans for business
- Bringing it all together

After you've completed each section of your business plan, make about four good-quality, full-color copies and assemble them.

Some choices for assembling your business plan are:

- Spiral binding (done at many office supply and copy stores)
- Plastic report cover binding
- Three-ring binder

Give your plan the polished look it deserves and don't cut corners in assembling the final product. You've worked hard to show that your business is solid. Present your material in an easily readable format with dividers for each section and with your full-color logo front and center.

The Least You Need to Know

- Writing a business plan is essential to any startup business.
- Your business plan is the road map outlining the decisions you have made and will make for your business.
- You can write a good business plan by working step by step through the sections of the plan.

Action Steps

- Start by writing a simple outline of your ideas for your business.
- Conduct market research on other area pet-sitting businesses.
- Write a mission statement.
- Write a vision statement.
- Begin putting together your projected financials.
- Write your business plan.

Sample Income Statement

Business Name

Income Statement
Date

Income

Pet Sitting Services	$234,927.64
Total Income	234,927.64

Expenses

Payroll	126,986.44
Payroll Taxes	32,220.89
Advertising & Promotions	8,590.32
Insurance	1,514.00
Pet Supplies	2,178.12
Professional Fees	6,130.63
Other Operating Expenses	5,025.17

Total Expenses 182,645.57

Net Income $52,282.07

05 Getting Started

By this point you've determined if a home-based pet-sitting business is for you. The challenges of busy holidays, early mornings, late nights, and the occasional puppy house-training mishap haven't deterred you and your determination. You are looking forward to making your own decisions about your business and where to go. Now let's get from point A to point B and get started! But getting started in the right way is essential. Many animal lovers have started pet-sitting businesses only to feel overwhelmed and either over-worked or underworked with no plan in place, no organization, and no idea of what to do. They end up being a part of the SBA statistics that predict that your business has about a 50-50 chance of surviving past five years. That is far better than the published numbers of past SBA surveys showing that only one in ten businesses will survive past five years. We definitely want to be the 50 percent that make it for the long haul, and getting started the right way, with the right tools and organization, is essential to your success. Winging it is not an option.

Congratulations! You are on your way to a successful home-based pet-sitting business. If you've skipped any of these steps and feel you are ready to

Checklist

You've come up with a business name and made sure you can use it.
You've registered your name with the county.
You've purchased your domain name.
You've completed your business plan.

Join one or both professional organizations related to pet sitting:
- Pet Sitters International (www.petsit.com)
- National Association of Professional Pet Sitters (www.petsitters.org)

open your business, stop. Do not proceed. Poor planning will lead you down the path of missed pet-sitting assignments, lost client keys or payments, missing tax forms, and the destruction of your business.

Become a Member of a Professional Organization

Both national pet-sitting organizations offer good tools for getting your business started and continuing education and support for their members.

Many pet sitters belong to both organizations to get the full benefit of both memberships. The value you get from joining at least one group is phenomenal. You will be able to easily purchase insurance and bond policies, gain access to members-only marketing materials, and use continuing education resources through their accreditation programs.

The Costs of Starting Your Business

You've already encountered some of the costs of starting up your new business like your county registration fees and your domain name purchase. Perhaps you've even looked into some of the costs of setting up your home and mobile office. The startup costs for most home-based pet-sitting businesses are extraordinarily low. In 1998 we started Cathy's Critter Care with an investment of about $400. When we started, though, there weren't any pet sitter–specific software programs to buy, the online referral service from national pet-sitting groups was just starting, and more people relied on using paper phone books or calling the home office of the national organization for a referral. We were able to start very small, very low cost and to grow slowly.

The situation has changed exponentially in the last ten to fifteen years in the pet-sitting business. Some of the costs have risen but not much. It's still entirely feasible to start your home-based pet-sitting business on less than $1,000—especially if you already have a computer and cell phone. There are definite ways to cut corners and really go low cost in starting a home-based pet-sitting business. It's not out of the realm of possibility to start with just a couple of hundred dollars and add expenses as you grow. You don't have to have software when you start out. Google calendars, Yahoo! calendars, Outlook, and iCal will all work just fine for keeping track of your clients when you start. Paper calendars work fine, too. Paper accounting methods are simple and easy for a startup business. Don't fall into the trap of thinking that you have to take out a loan to get started. You don't. You can start low cost. You shouldn't overextend yourself. As you grow, and you will, you can add software to handle your bookings and client information, you can add additional advertising and all the bells and whistles that make a thriving pet-sitting business hum.

Your Office

The pet sitter's office can consist of as little space as a spare closet set up with a computer and small file box and small safe where you keep your clients' keys and payments. As your pet-sitting business grows, you might need to expand that space (mostly for your clients' files and the many books you will inevitably read and want to keep). In addition, as you get busier, you will spend less time in your home office and more time in your mobile office—your car!

Some assumptions are made in setting up the home office as outlined next. The first assumption is that you will be conducting some of your business via e-mail/Internet with the use of a computer. This is not a necessity but is generally the norm for pet-sitting companies today. However, should you need use of the Internet, you can use your local library computers. Another assumption is that you will need some form of printing from your computer. Many pet-sitting businesses run a paperless system. This is a definite advantage and a good way to set yourself apart from other companies in your area, ride the wave of the green movement, and cut your costs as well. I would always suggest you keep hard copies of your client service agreements

Remember that to receive the IRS home-office tax deduction, the space you claim as your office must be solely used for that purpose. You can set up your office on your dining room table, but if it is not solely and completely set aside for your business activities, you might not be able to claim the home-office deduction. See www .IRS.gov.

and contracts, but many other areas of your business can be scaled back to virtually paperless production.

Your office will include:

- A work surface (table or desk)
- Chair
- Office supplies (paper, pens, pencils, paper clips, stapler)
- Computer
- Printer
- Phone (landline or cell)
- Two-drawer file cabinet or file box
- Key box (see Chapter 5 on keys)
- Small safe

We currently have about five hundred active clients (those who have used our service in the last twenty-four months) and have a full office set up in fifty square feet.

Your Website

Let's talk about your website for a minute. I am a firm believer that in today's market, if you are in business, you'd better have a website. You are going to be linked for free to an online referral service when you join one (or more) pet-sitting organizations/groups. In addition, there are other opportunities to link your website to other directories, and many of these are free, too. You just won't get the bang for your buck anywhere else. I am amazed at how many pet-sitting businesses still don't have websites at least outlining who they are, what they do, and why they should be chosen from the companies in their area.

Most home-based pet-sitting businesses will do fine with a template-based website. You don't need a custom-built site, which is where the mulithousand-dollar costs come into play. Many of the hosting or domain registration sites even offer free templates you can use. If you find a template and like the hosting plan, you can use it for your website building, too. Even if the template doesn't have a lot of options for pet pictures, you can use generic backgrounds and color schemes that suite your business. It's better to have a good, clean site with your basic information than to have nothing. Remember that if you build your site through one of the hosting or registration companies, your website belongs to them. If you discontinue service with them, you will not be able to move the website, in whole, the way it looks now to another provider. You might have to rebuild it. Intuit.com has a nice product that is easy to use and at the time of this writing even uses a dog-walking service as a business example.

Your website is your chance to put into your own words the who, what, why, and where of your pet-sitting business. It will work for you twenty-four hours a day, seven days a week and answer questions that potential clients have. Pictures are good on websites, but potential new clients come to your site to get information, so keep your website content rich. More on websites in that section of this book, but don't shortchange your business by not having a website. I so firmly believe in the power of a good website that I think it is more important than even T-shirts, business cards, and brochures.

Detailed information on what to include on your website and how it should look will be addressed in a separate section.

Spending Your Startup Dollars

The items listed next are arranged in relative importance. For example, if you only have x amount of dollars, go down the list with that money to start out and wait for the other expenses until you start generating an income. Or pick and choose what you think will best suit your business and overall structure as presented in your business plan.

The following are approximate costs. These may vary by locale and/or vendor. The costs are set up in annual expenses unless noted otherwise.

Dba license fee	$20 (one-time fee for several years)
Professional affiliation membership	$150 per organization
Insurance	$100
Bond	$50
Additional training in pet first aid/CPR	$60
Website (name purchase)	$10–$35
Website (hosting)	$60–$100
Website (building)	$0–$500
Client welcome home gifts	$250–$400
Business cards	$50
Office supplies/setup	$100–$500

Computer	$600 (one-time cost)
Internet service	$200–$600
Printer	$100 (one-time cost)
National convention	$300–$1,000
Pet-sitting software	$100–$600
Business T-shirts	$50–$200
Yellow Pages in print	$360–$5,000(+)

Many of these items, like your website building and business card printing, can be $0 if you are handy with HTML, Frontpage, or Dreamweaver and build your site and use some of the free resources for printing cards online! In addition, if you choose to use a template provided by your website hosting company, then your costs could be $0. You can even print cards and brochures on your home printer and get a fairly professional look. This is perfectly acceptable and a good way to lower your overall startup costs.

Professional Help from Attorneys, CPAs, and Marketing Gurus

We started CCC on a shoestring budget. We didn't advertise in the Yellow Pages (too expensive for a startup business). We didn't hire fancy marketing people to tell us what to do with the money we didn't have for marketing and advertising. We just did what we were good at. We talked to the people we knew about what we were doing, and we grew our business slowly but without debt. You don't need to hire anyone to help you with marketing or advertising. You need to put in the sweat equity you have available at no cost to you and go to pet fairs and adoption days and even join a dog exercise group; you don't need to pay expensive marketing specialists.

When I set out to write this book, I did so with the intent to give the information and guidance that worked for me in starting and growing CCC. At the time we started our pet-sitting business, we didn't have any expendable or saved income. We couldn't afford to hire an attorney, a CPA, or even an accountant. We read books checked out from the library and worked our way along until we had the resources available to hire the professionals we needed. You can do the same thing. The resources in this book will get you started and headed in the right direction. However, if you have investment money to spend on your business, a good use of that money is in consultation with both an attorney and a CPA who can give you advice on tax issues as well as answer accounting questions. Many of your accounting

Most of the pet-sitting software programs available for purchase (online or system based) include good accounting software when you are ready to use it. They all do a good job of keeping track of who has paid and by what method, and most can run reports showing you revenue by date, zip code, or even referral source.

questions will be answered later in this book, but the advice of a CPA can be tailored to your personal circumstances and your state's specific tax laws.

The national pet-sitting organizations have good recommendations on professional business services like legal contacts. This is a member benefit that you can take advantage of. After you are a member, you can link to these services and see if they're right for you. Some of the legal services offered by affiliates to the national organizations include:

- Legal consultation and advice
- Contract and document review
- Letters and phone calls
- IRS audit legal services
- Motor vehicle legal services
- Trial defense services

(Legal services reprinted with permission from Pet Sitters International)

Designing a Logo

Most businesses use a logo of some sort. Some logos are actually the product's name written in a specific font and format, and some logos are an additional graphic representation of the business. If you are creative and want to design a logo, then here's your chance to stretch your wings. A logo is good because at a glance people will start recognizing your business.

When designing your logo keep in mind:

- Reproducibility of the logo in both black-and-white and color. This becomes especially important if you need to have anything embroidered. The more detailed and complicated your logo, the more it will cost to reproduce and the trickier it will be to maintain the integrity of the logo.

A Testament to the Power of a Logo

We are currently working on a new project. A pet-care campus. During construction we've posted banners with just the outline of our logo and the words "Coming Soon . . ." Several of our clients have e-mailed and called to ask if we are building something because they thought for sure the logo on the banner looked like ours. There are no words in the logo on the banner. It is just an outline. That speaks volumes to the power of a logo. Without any words or even any of our company colors, our logo was recognizable.

- Overall company color scheme. If you don't like orange and teal, don't use it in your logo. Colors are immeasurably important to a logo. Choose your colors wisely.
- Ability to use the logo across many formats, including business cards, brochures, T-shirts, bumper stickers, car wraps, pet food can lids, pens, etc. You can see the many uses your logo will have.

The best logos incorporate about three colors and simple, classic designs. Silhouettes of pets work nicely because it's sometimes tricky to get the right-looking pet face. Whiskers, tails, and leashes added into your business name are a good simple option, too. Play around with some ideas and colors and get the opinions of your friends and family on what they like best.

Color is an important aspect of your logo, so choose wisely. You will use these colors across the board in your marketing and advertising campaigns as you start your business and continue through the years. If you choose a hue of teal as one of your colors, be prepared to use that on shirts, can lids, and other items. Be consistent with your colors, and you will quickly establish an identity. Demand that any printers you use be able to reproduce your business colors exactly. They should be familiar with a system of classifying colors known as the "pantone color system." This is a standardized color reproduction system using the CMYK (cyan, magenta, yellow, and black) process for printed materials and the RGB (red, green, blue) system for online reproduction. Good-quality printers and screeners will understand your desire to maintain your color scheme across the board.

> **Business Identity = Name + Logo + Colors**
>
> **From www.entrepreneur.com**
>
> Brand building is simply a new label for a collection of functions that have always been necessary to make a business successful, requiring ongoing effort in several areas to:
>
> - Increase the public's awareness of your business name and logo.
> - Build a strong company "essence" that inspires loyalty and trust in your current customers and provides a level of familiarity and comfort to draw in potential customers.

After you decide on your logo and colors, use them everywhere. Put them on your service forms, envelopes, and all stationery as well as all of your advertising items where possible. Look online for some ideas, and you will be rolling with ideas. Using your logo consistently and frequently will establish your business identity and brand quickly. People will recognize your mark before they even realize it consciously.

After you decide on a basic idea for your logo, you will need to digitize it in a format that printers can use like .jpg and .gif. If you have an idea of what you want but need some help digitizing it, look into the graphics design department at your local community college. You can even find graphic artists on Craigslist. They are generally less expensive to work with and more flexible than bigger agencies you would find elsewhere.

After you've begun using your logo, you can trademark/service mark it at the state level, and if you are providing pet sitting to more than one state, you can apply for a federal trademark. This will prevent anyone from using your logo or one similar to it for her pet-sitting business. You cannot trademark your logo until you've started using it, though. If your logo incorporates your business name as well, you might want to apply for two separate service marks. One for your name. One for the logo. That will prevent anyone from using your exact business name as well as the graphical representation of it. Remember that to find information on service marks, go to your state's secretary of state website.

Keys and Keys and Keys, Oh My!

Among the most important and sensitive items you will handle are your clients' keys. Keys are so important that they might need their own chapter. So much can go so wrong when you are dealing with keys to clients' homes. Clients depend on you to safely handle and maintain their keys. It is an essential component to home security. Your clients trust you to maintain their keys safely. If you fail to do so, you will quickly lose their trust and find yourself calling a locksmith to rekey a home (at a cost to you, of course).

You will need to set up a method by which you can reliably, comfortably, and reasonably keep track of:

- The keys you are currently using to service clients
- The keys for clients in your active files whom you aren't working for right now

You will need to handle keys for clients who for one reason or another haven't called you for care in a long time. Will you dispose of their keys? Mail them back? What if they've moved? These are all things you will need to address in your key policy so that everyone is on the same page. Be prepared to explain how you handle keys and what your clients' options are.

You have essentially three methods by which to safely handle keys:

1. Your clients maintain possession of keys between services. You pick up the keys and drop them off at the beginning and end of each service.
2. You maintain possession of your clients' keys during and between services.
3. Your clients maintain possession of keys and put them out for you in a lock-box each time they need care.

Whatever method you choose or any combination of these, remember:

"A loose key is a lost key!"

(Quote provided by Kim Tank, Apronstrings Pet Sitting) Have a designated pet-sitting keychain with a reliable keyring onto which you put all of your pet-sitting keys. Do not let keys sit loose in your car, in your pocket, on your desk, on your kitchen counter, or anywhere else. Remember this mantra (hopefully not while you are looking for a lost key).

Option 1: Your clients maintain possession of keys between services. You pick up the keys and drop them off at the beginning and end of each service.

When you are just starting up your business, or you plan to stay relatively small, you can choose to pick up keys from clients needing care each time they reserve their dates. Of your options, this is probably the least-used method by most professional pet sitters for handling keys but is certainly still a good option and one with many benefits.

There are some definite pros to this option. Your clients are responsible for their own keys, thus limiting the possibility of your losing an important key between services due to misfiling, mishandling, or just a mishap. In addition, if your clients know to expect to see you for a key pickup before they leave, this is a good check and balance to ensure that all the clients who have reserved care are on your schedule. If you haven't picked up their key, they are apt to call you and double check on their care! You have the opportunity to always make sure that the key you have is a good, working key. When you pick it up, you have the opportunity to check it immediately and not be left wondering why the key you had on file at the office isn't working only to find out that a client forgot to tell you that he had the locks changed since his last service! And lastly, this option gives you the perfect opportunity to pick up payment in full for services that are booked.

One of the major drawbacks to this method of handling keys is that it will require more of your daily time and possibly your biggest business expense: gas. Part of your scheduled appointments for a day will include key pickups and dropoffs, and as you start working, you will find that Benjamin Franklin's axiom, "Time is money," is true! There are only so many hours in a day, and eating those up with key pickup and dropoff appointments can cut into your financial bottom line.

Furthermore, clients like convenience! If you do not have their key on file, and they have last-minute needs, it might become a challenge to set up a time to get the keys from them. They are also not as bound to using your services as if you have a copy of their key. Of course, you want all of your clients to be extraordinarily happy with your care and to let you know if they are not. Let's be realistic and face the facts: It is much easier to call another pet-sitting service for care next time instead of addressing concerns with you directly if you do not have possession of their key. People tend to naturally take the path of least resistance and conflict. I am not saying that you should convey the sense of holding someone's key hostage, but with a

Recommended words to use when talking to clients about picking up and dropping off their keys each service: "I know how sensitive your home security is, so as a business, I've chosen to devote some time to each set of services to come to you and pick up your key shortly before your departure. This will give you the peace of mind in knowing that I've got a working key, that your services are on my calendar, and that there are no unnecessary copies of your keys not in your possession." If you decide to charge for this service, you can add: "On each set of services you will see a nominal fee for key pickup and key dropoff to cover the time and expenses associated with the service."

key on file, you are more likely to hear back from previous clients and have the option to address their concerns adequately.

It is not a good idea to have your clients "hide" a key for you to get on the first visit and leave back there on the last visit. There is a chance that they will forget to leave the key out for you, but more importantly, anyone might see them leave this key or otherwise find it. If you've told them to do this or recommended that they do this or left the key on your last visit, you might be held liable for any loss associated with this.

Most pet-sitting companies that require this method of key handling do not charge their clients for the pickup and dropoff. However, some companies do. It is your option to explain to your clients why you chose this method of handling keys and explain to them the necessity to charge for your time.

Option 2: You maintain possession of your clients' keys during and between services.

This is the most widely used option by professional pet sitters for handling keys. The biggest benefit of this method is that your time spent in picking up keys for care is greatly reduced, allowing you to focus your scheduling and time on pet sitting. You will pick up your client's keys (preferably two keys—see "Good Ideas", page 90) at the preservice meeting for a new client and keep them on file at your office for all future services. Additionally, you will not need to pass on any of the expenses associated with key pickups and dropoffs to your clients, limiting their extra costs for pet care.

Good Ideas

It's always a good idea to pick up two key copies from your client. You will have a backup if anything happens to the original key (keys have been known to be dropped down drainage openings in roads on a dog walk, through grates in city streets, etc.). Even if you must have the house rekeyed for security purposes, at least you will still have a backup key to gain entrance to the house while you continue care. It is also a good idea to have that extra copy in a place where an emergency backup person who is familiar with your office set up and business has access. If anything serious happens to you (car accident, medical or family emergency, or other issue), someone else will have access to your client keys and can maintain service!

Keep a door key for clients who want you to use a garage door opener or garage keypad to gain entrance. When the electricity is out, automatic garage doors won't work! Batteries have been known to go dead when the client is out of town, too. To avoid being stuck outside without any options, keep the client's key on your set of pet-sitting keys while providing care. A good idea is to use it the door key to gain entrance for the first visit on a set of services and have the client leave the garage door opener for you inside where you can pick it up and use it for the remaining visits. Then you can leave it for the client on the last visit with your visit notes and lock up the door behind you with the key. Don't volunteer to keep garage door openers between services. They are expensive to replace if lost or broken.

Holding client keys between services requires that you establish a reliable way to maintain and organize your clients' keys safely. As mentioned previously, you should use one, good, sturdy keyring for your current pet-sitting clients. Avoid filing a key with any client paperwork that would indicate where the client lives. You should also avoid writing the client's name on her key. Many pet sitters devise their own key codes. For example, some sitters use the first letter of the client's last name along with an internal numerical or alphabetical code not associated with the client's address (see "Coding Your Keys", page 91). When you label your keys, label the actual key, not a keyring attached to the key. Key tags can be flimsy, and inevitably the key will fall off of its ring.

You can find small white labels at many office supply stores. You can use the whole label or cut it in half. Write the client's code on the label, stick it to the key (one on each side is even better). Then, to have even more reassurance that the label will stay put and to keep the writing from wearing off as quickly, "seal" the label with clear tape around the entire top of the key so that it covers the labels on both sides. If you find yourself without a sticky label, use a small piece of regular paper. Write the client's code on the paper and tape one to each side. By wrapping tape around the flat part of the key, you will ensure that the label won't fall off.

Coding Your Keys

Assign a client code based on the month and year that the client started care with your company. In that way each time you work for that client, even ten years down the road, you will remember the date she started with you and reward her accordingly! Let's look at this: Jane Smith signed up for her first set of services with you in August 2010. Her key might have the following code attached: S0810 ("S" for "Smith," "08" for "August," "10" for year "2010"). If you have two clients who start care in the same month and have the same last-name initial, use a second or third letter of their name as long as you don't write their whole name on the key. Alternatively you could include the actual day of the month that you met with the client. So, Jane Smith, whom you met with on August 16, 2010, would have code S081610.

Option 3: Your clients maintain possession of keys between services. You issue them a lockbox that they put their key in when you leave.

This method is relatively new to the pet-sitting industry, but it works nicely. This is the method that works best for my business at this point. As your business grows, you might find that you move through the three key options as outlined here. That's okay. Do what works for you at the time but be flexible enough to know when your business model needs to shift a little bit.

Shurlock Lockbox for Your Clients' Key(s)

We've used Shurlock lockboxes for four years now and have had success with them. They are easy to use, reliable, and inexpensive. We pass the cost along to our clients when they sign on with care through CCC. There are some situations in which you cannot use a lockbox, primarily at apartment complexes.

Be flexible in what you can do for your clients but explain to them the benefits of using a lockbox for their keys:

- No unnecessary key copies are made for sitters.
- Unexpected emergencies or accidents for the sitter with your key aren't an issue. Your key is at your client's house.
- Your clients have a key to their home when they return even if they left their keys in Tahiti.

If you explain the pros of using the lockbox and explain to your clients that the box does not have to go on their front door like a Realtor lockbox does, most people will see the benefit. We charge a $20 deposit for the lockbox. If clients keep the lockbox forever, that's okay. If they move or discontinue service with our company permanently, they can return the lockbox to us and get $15 of their deposit back. The code on the lockbox can be reset to any numbers at any time, so they can be customized to meet your clients' needs and reused as long as they are in good condition.

This method might work well for your business as you expand into a larger service area or hire staff to help you with visits. Of course, there are still those Murphy's Law moments when clients have forgotten to put their lockbox out or left an incorrect key in it. But those are few and far between. With reminder e-mails and phone calls of service as part of your precare planning, these instances don't happen often. Clients enjoy being in control of their keys, and it removes the responsibility of keeping up with keys from you.

Your clients (or sometimes even colleagues) might tell you that they would be nervous about using a lockbox for their keys. They fear that it would alert people that they aren't home. Or they are worried that thieves would steal the lockbox to break into their home. We've found this not to be the case. As a matter of fact, we now keep a lockbox at our house, and it is out 365 days a year. We use it for those emergencies that leave us without access to our house. We've never had a lockbox stolen or had one inappropriately used to enter a client's home. If thieves want to break into a home, they can do it in easier ways than tracking down which houses may or may not have lockboxes. Just remember to be discreet with the location and with the numbers associated with the box.

Presenting Yourself to the Client

You knock on the door of your very first clients. It's time to meet their pets and them. It's okay to be nervous, but being prepared will help. A presentation book is a good tool to have with you at your meetings with clients. A 1-inch notebook with a sleeve cover into which you can insert a copy of your logo or at least your business name works great. As you progress and have more time under your belt, your presentation book will evolve and likely grow bigger. But it is an invaluable tool to have from the beginning. It not only holds the materials you show your clients to let them know you have set yourself apart from others but also is an easy way to carry the materials you need to complete the meeting with the client. It also gives you a writing surface on which to take notes at the visit. Your logo and business name should be on all of the materials in the book and definitely on any material you give to the client.

Your presentation book should include:

- Business cards and brochures you can give to your client
- Your business license after registering with the county
- Membership information for any professional groups to which you belong
- Professional certifications from additional training (certification, pet first aid and CPR)
- Thank you notes and referrals written by other clients
- Insurance and bond information
- Code of ethics or standards of practice for professional pet-sitting services*
- Any press releases for your business
- Pictures of you with your client's pets and your own pets and any other interesting pictures of you at community events and elsewhere—they speak a thousand words
- Handouts to give clients on topics such as heatstroke, hypothermia, bloat, dog-walking safety, good pet nutrition, and personal safety†
- Service agreement, policies, references

---

*These are easily obtained from either of the two national pet-sitting organizations after you join.

† Your clients might indicate any of these issues with their pets. Even if they don't, you can pick one, like personal safety when walking with dogs, and leave it for them. This will let them know you are serious about what you do.

Insurance and Bond Policies

You will need to acquire both policies. They are relatively inexpensive, and you should absolutely not operate without both policies in place. A bond policy usually covers a party outside the owner such as

> Insurance policies cover acts of negligence, and bond policies cover acts of dishonesty and theft.

an employee or independent contractor. Often it's not necessary to have a bond in place for an individual owner. However, a bond policy, whether required or not, gives your clients another source of security in knowing they've hired a true professional and can rest assured that should anything happen, you and they will be covered. It's a good idea to purchase the policy so that you can tell people your business is insured and bonded. You will save time by not having to explain why a bond isn't necessary and will bring additional clients to your business because it is an industry standard to have both policies.

It is important to obtain insurance from a company accustomed to the unique nature of pet sitting. Many companies offer policies that on first glance appear to cover the pet sitter adequately. However, because our services are provided in the client's home, there are sometimes gaps in coverage.

At minimum, you want an insurance policy that covers:

- Injury or illness to the pet
- Injury to people by the pet in your care
- Damage to the client's property in your care, custody, and control
- Coverage for lost or stolen keys

PSI and NAPPS both offer recommended providers of insurance and bond policies. These companies have proven their commitment to the pet-sitting industry over many years and have stood behind many sitters who've had claims filed against their business. These companies provide reliable coverage and are a safe purchase.

> Insurance does not cover injury or accident to pet sitters, their employees, or independent contractors. Insurance covers the client's property and pets against damage or loss.

There are additional sources of insurance as well. Several can be found on the Internet. Research the various options closely and choose the one that best meets your needs. Purchase your pet-sitter insurance before your first visit.

Insurance Options for Pet Sitters

- Pet Sitter Associates, LLC (www.petsitllc.com)
- Business Insurers of the Carolinas (www.petsitterinsurance.com)
- Mourer-Foster, Inc. (www.kennelpro.net)

Establishing your Policies

Part of setting yourself up as a professional is establishing business policies. It might be easy in the beginning to deal with last-minute bookings, cancellations, and trips to pet supply stores for food and litter, but they will quickly become a business killer if you continue to provide these types of accommodations for your clients as you get busier. Policies are tricky because generally speaking, the professional pet sitter is a kind, compassionate person, and sticking to the policies just doesn't come easy for us. However, establishing fair, clearly defined boundaries gives you and your clients the guidelines necessary to have a successful business relationship. The good thing about being the owner is that when extenuating circumstances pop up, you can bend the policies for a client in need.

Your policies should include:

Cancellation policy and fees (including early return policy)

Payment policy for new clients and existing clients (including return check fees)

Policy for visitors in the home

Late booking policies

Key policy

Policy for additional services (trips to vet and supply pickups)

Ready . . . Set . . . Go! Let the Press Know!

Never written a press release? Have no fear. They sound intimidating, like something that only a big business or journalist should use. Press releases will become key to your free advertising campaign and a tool you can retrieve from your marketing arsenal whenever you need to. Writing a press release is easy. There is a standard format that news agencies are accustomed to seeing. In order to be effective you will need to stick to this format.

When you write a press release, remember that you are submitting this information to a news agency looking for a story that will interest the reader (or in the case of radio and television, the listener and viewer). The fact that you opened a new business won't be interesting to them. It is interesting to you, but new businesses open every day.

For every press release you write, keep in mind that you will need to provide a story. Highlight something interesting and newsworthy about pets or the pet industry that will tie into your press release. Although the opening of your business might not be interesting and newsworthy to the general population, the fact that the pet industry is bigger than the toy industry in the United States is something interesting. The fact that about six out of ten homes have at least one pet and that pet owners are working longer hours to ensure their job in a shaky economy can tie into your pet-sitting business story in an effective and interesting way. Whatever the topic is that you want the reporter to cover, you will need to find an interesting tie-in. Then include what you want to highlight in the press release and offer an interview and pictures to complete the story. If you write a good press release, you will have essentially written a good story and done the reporter's job for him or her. This will get your information turned into a news story.

The last paragraph in the body of your press release is called the "boilerplate." This is a brief synopsis of your pet-sitting business and you. This will be something that stays fairly consistent in all of your press releases.

At the end of the body of the press release, include "###." This is standard press release format.

Lastly, include a paragraph stating that you can be contacted for further information, interviews, and pictures.

Always write a press release in third person, like you are writing a news story. The body of your press release should be three to five short paragraphs but should always fit on one page. Be sure to include quotes from yourself so they can be included in the actual news story.

Press releases are easily distributed by e-mail and fax, making them a fast way to send information. Your first press release will announce your business' opening. Use press releases in the future to announce:

- Participation in local events
- Attendance at conventions and regional meetings
- Important anniversary dates for your business
- Expansion of your business with hirings or service area increases

You can use a press release to announce anything happening in your business. Remember to write a press release highlighting a newsworthy pet topic and tie in your quotes and business information. Reporters really don't care about promoting your business or telling people about your great customer service skills or making you money. They want an interesting story that their readers will enjoy. The better you present the information they can use right away, the more likely you are to get your story in print. Putting a local touch to your news story will often get your release noticed.

Send your press release at the optimal time. If there is a national event happening or local crisis that is taking up a lot of news time and coverage, wait to send your press release until things have calmed down. Generally it is best to send press releases midweek. You can find press release fax numbers on the website of most major news publications. Compile a list of all of the media outlets you want to send your release to and look up their fax number for press releases. This document is commonly called a "media list." If you have a contact at the local newspaper or neighborhood magazine/newsletter, send your press release directly to that person for a better chance at coverage. Don't get discouraged if you don't hear from someone after your first attempt. Send out another press release, and eventually you will get the hang of writing a good release and get noticed.

The Least You Need to Know

- Joining one of the national pet-sitting organizations is well worth the cost and will get you access to many member benefits designed to help with starting your business.
- Home-based pet-sitting businesses can be started with low costs. Services like pet-sitting software to manage your business can be added later. The must-haves before you start pet sitting are business name registration with

the county, membership in one of the national organizations, and your insurance and bond policies.

- A pet-sitting business can be set up in a home office as small as just a spare closet or corner of the room. Your office will take up minimal space.

- Your best tool to advertise your business is a website. Simple websites will give potential clients the information they are looking for and will inspire them to call you for care. You will be able to link your website to a locator database through many of the pet-sitting organizations.

- Professional help from attorneys, marketing firms, and CPAs is not a necessity at the beginning of your home-based pet-sitting business.

- Designing a logo and setting up a color scheme for your business will help you begin your branding process.

- Finding a key system that works for you is a must. You have options on how to handle client keys and who maintains possession of the keys.

- Putting together a presentation book for your business will help you convey to new clients as well as other business contacts your professional status.

- Know what you are buying when you purchase insurance and bond policies. Coverage can vary from company to company, so make certain the coverage is what you need to protect your business and clients.

- Policies are a necessity for any business. Policies will give you and your clients a clear picture of what is expected and get everyone on the same page.

- Well-written press releases can serve as a powerful marketing and advertising tool for your business.

Action Steps

- Join a national pet-sitting organization.
- Purchase business insurance and a bond policy.
- Set up your office space.
- Design your logo and pick your colors.
- Determine your key policy.
- Start putting together your presentation book. More will be added later.
- Write your business policies.
- Write a press release.

Money Talks
Finances, Financial Planning, Making a Profit, and Paying Your Taxes

Setting Up Your Bank Accounts

For tax purposes and accounting accuracy, you will need to set up business accounts at your bank or credit union separate from your personal accounts. If you've registered your sole proprietorship with the county and received your dba paperwork, or if you've set up your business as an LLC or incorporation and received your articles of incorporation, you will need to take those to the bank with you. It's a good idea to call the institution first and ask what documents and identification are required to open a business checking account and business savings account so you can go in prepared. You will probably need to take your driver's license or other form of picture identification.

Open the following accounts:

- Business checking account (with business debit card)
- Business savings account (to set aside estimated tax withholdings)
- Business savings account (emergency fund with three to six months' living expenses)

Clients should write checks to your business name only (the name that appears on your bank/credit union checks and statement). Refrain from accepting checks written to you personally.

When you purchase items for your business, write a business check or use your business debit card. Keeping your funds separate is essential in good business accounting. Your business debit card can be used instead of your business checks for any business expenses, including travel, and in most instances will give you the same protection offered by using a credit card. Debit cards will draw the money directly from your business checking account and avoid your overextending yourself with expenses that you cannot pay for.

In addition to your business debit card, you should consider applying for a no-fee credit card in your business name that you can use should you ever need to pay for emergency care for a client's pet and the client cannot be reached for payment.

Revenue—Setting your Prices

In your market research you learned about other pet-sitting businesses that are in your area and how much they charge for some of the services you will offer. Your research gave you a good idea of what other people are charging (fair market price), but does that mean that's what you should charge, too? In a capitalist economy, the producer of a good or service and the consumer ultimately determine the market price. This fact of business goes back to the laws of supply and demand. Generally speaking, the lower priced a needed good or service is, the more demand there is for that service. As the price goes up, the demand for the service decreases. These ideas can't be completely explored in this book because they call for lengthy discussions of economics. Good resources on basic economics both in the library and on the Internet will help explain supply and demand laws. What you need to know are the market value for pet sitting and the profit margin you want for your service.

> **You have to take into account several factors before determining your price for service.**
>
> - What is the value of your time?
> - How much overhead/expense do you have?
> - Would you rather do more visits with less profit margin or fewer visits with higher profit margin (one of the four p's of marketing—price)?

What Is Your Time Worth?

If you are leaving another job, it might be fairly easy to determine your hourly wage value. Suffice it to say that pet sitters don't make the hourly wage that attorneys do, but usually your wages should be more than what you could make working for someone else and should be commensurate with what other pet professionals like dog trainers and groomers make and should reflect your professional status, training, and any additional certification you have. An important fact to keep in mind is that if you are set up as a sole proprietor, you will pay approximately 25 percent of your earnings or profit to the IRS in the form of self-employment tax.

Total visit price - expenses = visit profit
Visit profit - tax liability = net profit

Don't mistake your gross visit profit as your hourly wage or net profit. You will have to deduct your taxes first.

Determining Your Expenses per Visit

Many of your expenses, as you discovered in writing your business plan, are fixed expenses. After you purchase your insurance for the year, that price is fixed for that year (note that some insurance policies determine your rate for the year based on your gross revenue from the year before, but for the current year, your price is fixed). Your telephone service is likely a fixed charge (as long as you don't go over on cell phone minutes), and your Internet service, web hosting, and your annual membership in a national organization are fixed as well.

To determine your expenses in providing a visit, add up all of the associated costs or expenses of providing pet sitting and divide that by the number of visits completed. This is usually easiest to do on a monthly basis. This number will fluctuate, going up in cost as the number of visits you complete goes down and vice versa. You should be able to establish a range of costs associated with providing care.

Sum of total expenses / number of visits = expense per visit
Expense per visit + travel cost = total expense of visit

The travel cost for most pet sitters is usually the cost of fuel required to get you to the client's home. See "Determining Fuel Costs" pages 112-113 for a complete explanation.

Summary of Some of the Business Expenses to Be Included in Your Calculations

- Advertising
- Bank charges
- Professional fees (accounting/legal/clerical)
- Business cards and brochures
- Business clothing
- Printing/photocopying
- Software computer service
- Fax supplies
- Online service charges
- Gifts and greeting cards
- Legal and professional services
- Office expenses and supplies
- Postage
- Continuing education
- Telephone expenses
- Computer/Internet expenses
- Association/organization dues
- Liability insurance
- Bond
- Books
- Magazine subscriptions

What Is the Profit Margin?

The last item in the revenue list (see page 100) is important to both you and your clients. When you determine your price and your philosophy on profit margin, keep in mind that it is okay to position yourself in the market with either approach. There isn't a right answer. This is something you will decide and move forward with. It is your business decision whether you will provide more visits and have a lower profit margin or do fewer visits with a higher profit margin. You will likely gain more clients with a lower price, but keep in mind that your overall value per hour of work is lower. You will have to see more clients than you would if your price, and thus profit margin, were higher. It is equally okay to set your prices higher and know that you will not meet the needs of as many potential clients, but you will have to provide fewer visits to make the same overall profit.

With these scenarios, you can see that pricing plays an important role in your overall business decisions. Will you provide lower-cost service to gain new clients and increase your overall client base (and often referral base as well)? Or will you start by offering a more exclusive service on the higher end of the price spectrum? In some way, the laws of supply and demand help determine what the right price is for a service. Keep in mind that as price goes up, demand generally goes down and that in the middle lies a common ground of high profitability. Some established pet-sitting businesses will say that they are busier than they would like to be but

Let's assume the following numbers for demonstration purposes:
Low price in your market is $14 per thirty-minute visit.
High price in your market is $19 per thirty-minute visit.

Scenario A: You decide to establish yourself in the market with a low price and choose to offer your service for $14 per thirty-minute visit. After your expenses, you make $7 per thirty-minute visit completed. Because clients in your target market are seeking a lower-cost alternative to their current pet-care costs, you book one hundred visits for a given amount of time. Your profit after these one hundred visits is $700.

Scenario B: You decide to establish yourself in the market with a better position and to be more available to clients with last-minute needs by not being as busy but offering your thirty-minute visits at $19 and recouping a $10 profit per visit. (Keep in mind that your cost per visit increases as the number of visits you make decreases.) Because you are higher priced, you do not gain the business of every person who calls for care. In fact, up to three out of ten people choose to purchase service from another pet-sitting company. You book seventy new visits in the same given amount of time. Your profit is $700, the same profit you made on completing one hundred visits.

When I started pet sitting, I provided a thirty-minute visit for $7.50. Even in 1998 that was on the low end of the market value for pet sitting, but the industry wasn't as widely known then, there weren't accreditation programs and continuing education, and we were battling the kid-down-the-street attitude about pet sitting. Setting my prices low allowed me to establish a base clientele who referred me to friends and family and gave me the foundation of referrals I needed to expand my business. As I got busier (and more experienced), I increased my prices gradually over time. Because I was established with my existing clients who signed on when prices were lower, they stayed with us for the most part. We knew we would lose some people, and we did, but that was okay because we were doing fewer visits for the same amount of profit. We eventually were (and are) priced on the upper end of our market.

continue to offer their services at the low end of the market price range. As you establish yourself and become a leader in the market, an expert in your field, and busier than you want to be, raising your prices is an acceptable business practice. You will be making the same amount of money for less time on the road.

Does Price Determine Quality? It's All in Our Head

There is one other factor to consider when setting your price. The psychology of consumers and how they associate your price with perceived quality determine a good portion of how they view your service. Have you ever paid more for an item because it was higher priced, and thus the perceived quality of the item was higher? Think about designer jeans, wine, and even generic versus name brand sodas, cleaners, and other items. Many consumers of goods and services determine perceived value (whether it is a conscious decision or not) by the price of the product. There is a well-documented psychological interaction between price and perceived quality that applies not only to goods but also to services. If your pet sitting is priced too low, there might be a perception of lower quality. You don't want people to think you offer less, are less dependable, or are overall a lower-quality service because you are priced too low.

Publishing Prices

Now that you've determined your price per visit and the pricing for your other services, how will you publish those prices? It's often debated whether to publish your prices or to have clients call you so that you can explain the care they get with your pet-sitting business. I am a firm believer in letting people know at least a general idea of what your charges are, if not specifying exactly what each item costs. When people are looking for a pet-sitting service, they want to know the price or at least a price range. They have choices, and if given a choice between a pet-sitting business that is forthcoming with pricing and one that is somewhat secretive and possibly perceived as hiding its pricing, they are likely to choose the business that gives them an idea of what to expect.

With the accessibility of the Internet, publishing and updating prices are easily accomplished without changing printed material and limit calls to your office from people looking for care at a cost that you can't provide. People don't need to be sold on all the bells and whistles that come with your care. They want to know if they can afford it and what is offered. This is easily accomplished at your website.

You don't want to spend money on printed materials detailing pricing only to have to change your prices for one reason or another and be left with inaccurate printed material. Be forthcoming with your prices on your website. Avoid putting your prices on printed material that might not be accurate in the future. Use brochures and business cards to drive people to your website. You can list all the services included in your pet sitting and establish yourself as a qualified pet sitter, thus cementing the value of your price. Include an easily found "Services and Rates" page on your website. Your potential clients will appreciate the fact that you respect their time in giving them the information they need. If you've done your research in pricing, you will be in line with what is a fair market value for pet sitting. One of the issues that some pet sitters have with putting their prices on their website is the inevitable exceptions that come with pet sitting. Not all three-pet households require the same work, and you don't want to get locked into a firm quote when there are exceptions to the rule. You can avoid these situations with a clearly written statement on your website that appears with your pricing plan letting clients know that the pricing is an estimate only and that for you to properly provide a quote for care, they should e-mail or call your office to discuss the details of their pet care.

Whatever your decision is about publishing your prices, you eventually will have to deal with the price shopper who might be looking for the cheapest option

I've had some great experiences working for neighbors and some really bad experiences as well. Knowing your emotional boundaries is essential when caring for neighbors' pets (as well as those of friends and family). One of the biggest benefits of hiring a professional pet sitter is that although a caring relationship is established, it is still one of a business nature. When you pet sit for friends, family, and neighbors, if anything goes wrong, you have lost not only a client but also a valuable relationship. In addition, people with whom we have a close relationship tend to blur the lines of what should and shouldn't be expected of a professional pet sitter. Use caution if you decide to work for people with whom you already have a personal relationship or who live in your neighborhood. It can make driving by that particular house a reminder of what might have gone wrong, and neighborhood picnics can become an uncomfortable reminder.

possible for pet sitting. Rest assured that through your research and work in determining your price, you've established a fair price for your pet sitting. Avoid letting people talk you into discounts for one reason or another. They will try. You want to avoid the pitfall of discounting your pet sitting. If you discount for one person, his friend will ask, too, and before you know it, you are providing discounts to a majority of your clients. Usually the price shopper isn't looking for the best care, just the cheapest. Set yourself apart from any competition by sticking to your pricing and reiterating that your business provides the quality care that the price reflects.

Be ready for neighbors to ask for a cheaper rate than is published. There are two sides to consider when dealing with neighbors. You can discount the cost of transportation and charge them only for your time, or you can stand firm on your price to avoid confusion should they refer someone they know and inadvertently give them the wrong price.

Invoicing and Payment

Your clients will want to know how and when to pay you. Now is the time to decide. Will you accept only cash? Will you accept cash, checks, credit cards, or a combination of any of these? Some pet-sitting businesses accept only credit or debit card payments so their accounting system can be fully automated and payments can be processed methodically and easily.

Most service industry businesses take all forms of payment. Options for you to accept credit and debit cards are offered through the national pet-sitting organizations, and you can even coordinate with some of the pet-sitter software on the market or services such as Paypal. Many clients enjoy the convenience and security of payment by credit card. It makes taking and receiving payments easy for you and your client. In addition, paying by credit card gives clients the added security of knowing that should you not follow through with your contractual obligation, they have some protection.

However, all credit card–processing options involve some costs, and these vary widely, so be sure to explore all of your options before committing to a processing

Every generation of smart phones seems to get just a little smarter. Now some phones even offer scanners and credit card–processing right through the phone. If you are a tech-savvy pet sitter, don't discount the wow power of using the latest and greatest tech tools to make your pet-sitting business even more successful. According to Amy Buttell's article in *Merchant Account Guide* (www.merchantaccountguide.com), "Users of iPhone, Palm Treo, HP iPAQ, Sprint Moto and other phones can purchase credit card processing applications that allow them to take credit card payments and transmit them securely without any carrying add-on magnetic stripe readers or other technology. These applications free merchants from their offices, land-lines and special processing equipment, potentially making business easier for merchants and employees who frequently work remotely. The applications are part of a broad-based effort by smart-phone manufacturers and application developers to push more business-related functions to all-in-one smart phones, making them more attractive to business owners and corporations." These applications work like other online credit card–processing software, and no swiping of the card is needed.

However, there is a hardware device that allows you to swipe a card and avoid having to enter the secure information into your phone. According to Michael Kwan of *Mobile Magazine* (www.mobilemag.com), the Square allows you to "swipe the card, the customer signs his or her name, and it's done. There's even an option to add a tip. A receipt is sent immediately via SMS or e-mail." This is a great convenience in the pet-sitting world where our face-to-face interaction with a client is out of our office.

option. You will want to use a credit card–processing system that transmits the charge through an online source like Authorize.net. Avoid buying any equipment for credit card swiping because you won't be using this equipment because clients don't come to your place of business. Several systems use keyed-in information to process the credit card.

Payment can be taken:

- In full at the beginning of service
- Half up front and half at the end of the service
- All at the end of service when the client is home and happy

There is no right or wrong way, and it is important to weigh the pros and cons of each option and do what is best for you and your clients. Make sure that in your policies and in regular communications with your clients you let them know how you handle payments. Some clients might have used another business that handled payments differently, so keeping them apprised of your payment policy is a good business practice.

Some clients are nervous about paying up front in full because they know that some unscrupulous businesses out there will take advantage of people. This concern is usually the case only with new clients who haven't used your pet-sitting service before. They might be worried that they will be dissatisfied with the care given and have no recourse to get their money refunded. If you opt to take payment up front, be prepared to explain to your clients that you understand their hesitation and that you want them to feel secure in knowing that your business is established, you are a member of one of the national pet-sitting organizations, and are insured and bonded. Most pet sitters are established residents in the community as well. If that's the case, mentioning that is helpful, too. Taking payment from a new client at the initial meeting has become an industry standard, so it isn't out of the norm. It also protects you from last-minute cancellations from new clients you've already devoted your time to getting set up for care.

Some clients feel better leaving payment up front if you offer to hold on to their check until they return home and can let you know they are happy with care. You can offer that they postdate the check for the day of their return.

It's usually easiest for your established clients to leave payment for you to pick up at the beginning of a service term when paying with cash or check. However, during especially busy times like holidays, you might request that your clients prepay for their reservation by mailing in a check or using their credit card. The last thing you want to deal with is last-minute cancellations at Christmas when you've already turned away other people who could have used those now-cancelled and unused slots.

If you are more comfortable taking only half the payment up front or waiting until the end of services, your clients will likely feel very comfortable with this approach, but know that you are accepting additional risk in not getting paid what you are due or wasting time sending reminders and making trips to pick up payment. It takes only one bad apple to spoil the whole bunch in this case. Some people out there will take advantage of your business and not pay you at all or take an extraordinarily long time to do so.

If you are clear about what your policies for payment and your reasons behind them are, most people will understand. I work only for clients willing to pay their full invoice at our initial client meeting and thereafter prior to their departure or by no later than their first visit during a service time frame. We lose some people because

An Excerpt from Cathy's Critter Care Policies

Payments

For all nonholiday bookings, payment is due in the form of a check, Visa, MC, Discover, or cash by no later than the beginning of service. Credit card payments should be called in to the office. Checks and cash can be left for your pet sitter to pick up on the first visit, or you may choose to mail your payment to:

[Your Business Address]

NEW CLIENTS will be required to pay for the full amount of services booked at the preservice visit.

RETURNED CHECK FEE = $30. Returned checks must be paid within three days after notification of return. Failure to pay the full amount due plus the returned check fee will result in additional late charges as outlined above and recourse through the district attorney's office for theft by check.

I won't budge on my payment policies, but I am willing to accept those losses and move on knowing that there might be some additional reason they didn't want to pay for services up front. You might avoid a long headache by setting your standards to ease your risk.

Clients Who Don't Pay

As mentioned, it takes only one client who doesn't pay to make you want to get a full credit report on anyone wanting to hire you. Most people are honest and happy to pay for a job well done. However, you will have to chase down some people if you want to be paid. Friendly notes worded as a polite reminder are your first step. Offer to swing by and pick up payment. By setting up your payment policies in the beginning to protect yourself, you can avoid the hassles of small claims court and collection agencies trying to get payment from a wayward client.

If a client writes you a bad check, you should notify her in writing and with a phone call. Most clients will rectify the situation promptly, but should you run into a problem collecting on a check that didn't clear due to insufficient funds, a closed account, or other banking problem, you have protection from these scenarios through your local district attorney's office. Check with that office to determine the procedures necessary to file a theft-by-check complaint.

Keeping Track of Payments

When you start your business, your accounting will be simple enough for you to handle. You will need to make certain that the clients you've worked for have paid you and keep track of those payments both for your record keeping and for IRS purposes. Following is a simple chart that you can build on any spreadsheet program to

Even in the times of plastic payments and online banking, people will still pay you in cash. It's tempting when you have $150 or more in greenbacks to just use it for spending money without reporting it. You always want your business to be completely aboveboard, so be sure to report your cash payments just like you would any other payment in your payment log. You can still spend the money without actually depositing it into your bank account as long as you've accounted for the payment internally and reported it as income.

help with this task. I used this accounting method for the first five years of my business. Each time you book a client to your calendar, you will need to write her name on the chart and enter her booked dates for services and the total amount due. When you receive payment you will fill in the last three fields. In "Payment Method" you will enter cash, check, money order, or the credit card used. Wait until you actually receive the payment before logging it in. At a glance you can see who hasn't paid you for care and remind them to do so. You can also total your receipts for any given period. I kept my income log in hard copy form, but you can certainly keep an electronic file (just be sure to use some form of backup in case your computer crashes) and print it monthly. If you build your file in a spreadsheet, you can even put in a formula to sum the total due and total paid columns for you.

Client Name	Dates of Service	Total Due	Payment Method	Date Received	Total Paid

How Much Money Is Your Business Making?

After you've determined how much revenue has come into your business (your gross revenue), you will need to subtract what you've spent on the business for the same time frame. Usually the best scenario is a monthly profit and loss statement. The profit and loss statement or a P&L as it is sometimes referred to as (see page 114) will show you how much money your business actually made in net taxable income. Remember when you prepared your financial statements for your business plan and worked off of your projection-based income and expenses? You might also recall that I mentioned it is wise to keep track of your income monthly and that becoming comfortable with the income statement is imperative. The profit and loss statement is also known as an "income statement." Small service-based businesses can use the single-step format for calculating their P&L, as discussed next.

For fixed expenses like insurance paid over the course of the year, divide the total annual payment by twelve to get your monthly obligation. Expenses that vary month to month are entered in a separate category. Some items for your business, like your phone expense, may be a fixed expense. If you have a month when your bill is different from normal, you can always move that to the other expenses category. Remember to include items such as monthly banking charges, too. Tailor the outline of the P&L to meet your business needs. The main point of the P&L is to use your total revenue/income and your business expenses to get you the bottom line, net income of your business. This number is important because it also represents your taxable income. If you are set up as a sole proprietor (and usually an LLC), you will need to set aside approximately 25 percent of your net income as your tax liability.

Keeping Up with Expenses

It is inevitable that you will have to pay taxes on the money you earn pet sitting. It is your legal duty to pay the taxes you owe. By keeping up with your expenses consistently, you can ensure that you are paying only the amount due by you and have deducted your costs of doing business from the revenue that you've received. Keep a good record of your expenses daily. A great tool to include in your mobile office (your car) is a receipt catcher for your car. When you make a purchase or pay a parking fee or toll, you can easily put the receipt into the holder and record a note for the expense. When it's time to do your monthly accounting for your P&L, you will transfer your expenses from your receipt log to your P&L expenses and check off that you've done so. Because the pet sitter is a mobile professional, having something with you will help you keep track of your purchases. Too many times receipts get lost in wallets and washed in pants pockets.

Your Biggest Expense

Here's how to get a grasp on estimating gas expenses. Stick with me here. After you get this concept, you will easily be able to figure your gas costs for any given client. This is important in figuring out what your fair price for care might be if a client lives outside your standard service area or if you need to go up on your rates based on increases in gas prices. The math that follows might seem like a long process to go through just to figure out this expense, but gas is going to be your biggest expense by far, so let's get an accurate account of that expense so that we aren't losing money. Here we go.

Determining Fuel Costs

Figure out how many miles per gallon your car gets first. How? Fill up your car. Top it off completely and note the odometer reading. Write it down either on the receipt, in a log book, or on a sticky note you can put in your console. Drive around town for a day or more. Just go about your normal routine. You might do a lot of city driving, rural driving, or a combination of both. After your tank is at least half empty but before you run out of gas, fuel up again and completely top off the tank. Get a printed receipt or note the exact number of gallons you just put into your car. Note the odometer reading this time and write it down.

Odometer reading 2 - odometer reading 1 = total miles driven

Total miles driven / total gallons to fill vehicle on second fillup = total MPG (miles per gallon)

The actual math might look something like this:

52,336–51,998 = 338 total miles driven

338 miles / 12.518 gallons = 27.001 miles per gallon

This tells you how many miles you can drive on one gallon of gas. So, according to the math we just did, your car gets 27 miles per gallon. How much will it cost you in fuel alone to see a client who lives 16 miles round trip from you? Gas at the time of fillup costs $3.29 per gallon. So, it costs you $3.29 to travel 27 miles.

16 miles (travel round trip for client) / 27 = 0.59 gallons of gas used

0.59 gallons x $3.29 = $1.95

With the preceding scenario, it will cost you $1.95 in fuel costs alone to see a client who resides 8 miles from you with the MPG your car gets and the current price of gas.

Now take the time to insert the real numbers into the equations and calculate your cost for a client x miles from you.

Be sure to keep an accurate record of the mileage driven for your business. It is your biggest tax deduction at the end of the year. Keep a journal or notebook in your car and record the mileage consistently. You will need to record the:

- Date
- Starting and ending odometer readings
- Total miles driven
- Purpose of trip (client's name is usually sufficient)

An entry in your journal might look something like this:

4/12/10 52,776 – 52, 881 105 miles post office, Smith, Jones, Gray (a.m. visits)

Profit and Loss Statement			
[dates]			
Cash			$
Check			$
Credit cards			$
Other			$
Monthly Fixed Expenses			
Home office			$
Insurance			$
Bond			$
Memberships			$
Internet			$
Phone			$
Other expenses			$
Gas/mileage			$
Phone			$
Postage			$
Office supplies			$
Gifts			$
Food/entertainment			$
Income − Expenses =			

Gross revenue/income − expenses = net profit or net loss

Most startup businesses do not have to submit quarterly tax payments until after the first year that the businesses show a profit. However, it might be a good idea to do it anyway. If your business is successful the first year and shows a profit, the last thing you want to have happen is to be short the money to pay your IRS obligation. If you can consistently set aside 25 percent of your earnings and know that you won't touch it, then you can pay your liability at the end of the year with your personal tax return. After your first profitable year, you will likely need to pay your taxes quarterly, so keeping a good record of your true net profit is essential.

It is important to properly store all of your business documents for any research that needs to be done by any taxing authority. After the year has ended and you've filed your taxes, compile all of your income sheet logs, bank statements, receipts, and all other financial documents into one neat packet and tightly rubber band them together with a copy of your tax return. Label them appropriately and store them safely. The jumbo (two-gallon) zippered plastic storage bags work well for

This book does not provide the scope necessary to give legal or accounting advice. It is best to check with the IRS as well as your state and local taxing authorities for information pertaining to your particular location.

The IRS has gone virtual. Striving to meet the needs of the small business owner, the IRS now offers online virtual workshops. According to the IRS, these workshops "are designed to help small business owners understand and meet their federal tax obligations."

The first three lessons are:

1. What you need to know about federal taxes and your new business
2. How to set up and run your business so paying taxes isn't a hassle
3. How to file and pay your taxes using a computer

Other lessons give instruction on running your business out of your home and setting up a retirement plan for yourself (and eventually your employees).

For this virtual workshop and others, visit www.IRS.gov/virtualworkshop.

If you can't find someone you are comfortable with, try online at www.natptax.com (National Association of Tax Professionals). The website also has information on allowable and overlooked deductions and other timely information on tax topics.

storage because they keep bugs and moisture from getting to your valuable business documents.

If preparing your own taxes makes you want to crawl into the dog house, then consider hiring a professional to prepare them for you. You won't need a CPA to prepare your taxes, but do look for a tax preparation service that has a solid reputation and is familiar with filing for small businesses. If you know of other small business owners in your area, ask for referrals. Too many preparers are not sufficiently trained in the changes to the tax code and can blindly lead you down the wrong path.

You might opt for using a tax-preparation software product like Turbo Tax (www.turbotax.com), H&R Block at Home (www.HRBlock.com), and TaxAct (www.TaxAct.com). These software programs have improved over the last several years and are great at walking the business owner step by step through all the income and deductions allowable by law. In addition, if you need explanation or

Don't forget to include the purchase of a tax software program or the use of a tax-preparation service in your business expenses.

help, the programs provide the resources to explain taxes in an easily understandable way. Each year the software is updated with the ever-changing tax codes, and the convenience of doing your taxes at home in your pajamas is quite a bonus. If you need to search a bit for a receipt, it's easily done.

Running Your Pet-Sitting Business Debt Free

As you can probably tell from the other sections in this book, I am a huge proponent of not overextending yourself financially when starting your pet-sitting business. What was once a dream and a blessing can become a nightmare and a curse if you aren't able to pay your debts from your earnings. This is especially true if you are a sole proprietor. There is no need to purchase huge Yellow Pages advertising and billboards, hire expensive firms, or invest in car wraps, fancy signs, etc. We will examine grassroots marketing techniques that get you the most bang for your buck (some with no cost) in the next chapter. Enough pet owners are looking for reliable care from a trustworthy and likable professional that you don't have to incur costs outside your initial investment and budget.

When you start seeing profits on your monthly P&L statements, invest a portion of those profits back into your business in the form of additional materials needed like pet-sitting software, T-shirts with your business name on them, and other items that will grow your business. Eventually you will see a big enough profit to invest in larger forms of advertising, and if you want to grow your business, you can afford to hire additional help in the form of employees. Don't fall into the trap of burdening your new business with too much financial debt. With the minimal supplies needed and the low cost of overhead for a home-based pet-sitting business, going into debt with credit cards, a line of credit, or home equity loans shouldn't be a consideration. Be patient. Grow slowly and steadily.

More Insurance!

Health and Disability Coverage

You've got a handle on your business insurance, but what about insuring you? You will be an integral part of your home-based business, and because you will be responsible for running the business, it's important to be sure that in case something happens to you, the income from your business isn't completely diminished or that if you need a medical procedure, you aren't left bankrupt because you don't have health insurance. If you are starting your pet-sitting business and have insurance through another employer or through your spouse's employer, you should keep that policy current. Health insurance for self-employed individuals is one of the most expensive policies. With changes in the health-care industry in recent years, prices have continued to rise.

The Health Care Reform Bill of 2010 is changing the landscape of insurance options available to the small business owner. Be sure to research current options and plans.

If you have no coverage for yourself or your family and are in generally good health, you might consider one of the high-deductible health plans (HDHP) that works in conjunction with an HSA (health savings account) plan. This gives you coverage for the lowest premiums possible,

Some nicely done clips explaining some health-care questions are on YouTube. Search for "staysmartstay hea1thy" (*NOTE:* the "l" is a numeral 1) in the YouTube search box.

allowing you to save the additional money you would be paying for premiums in a health savings account. These plans come with deductibles from $2,500 to $10,000 annually so they are not for individuals who are frequently ill or require ongoing medications or treatments. They will, however, do a good job of covering you if you encounter a major health crisis or catastrophic injury or illness. The philosophy behind the high-deductible HSA plans is that if you are relatively healthy, the money you would have spent on a higher premium and lower deductible would have been wasted if coverage wasn't needed. With an HSA the money in the account belongs to you and can often be transferred or rolled over to another HSA if you change carriers. In a sense, you are self-insuring up to your deductible amount and even more. It becomes your own health insurance for smaller costs and your deductible if you need one. HSA funds do not expire at the end of a given time period like FSAs (flexible spending accounts) from other plans do. They also grow a little through interest earned on the money in the HSA. Conceivably an HSA account could even be saved and used for medical expenses in the distant future, even in retirement.

According to cnnhealth.com in a report detailing a study in the *American Journal of Medicine*, over 60 percent of bankruptcies are caused by medical bills. "Unless you're a Warren Buffett or Bill Gates, you're one illness away from financial ruin in this country," says lead author Steffie Woolhandler, M.D., of the Harvard Medical School, in Cambridge, Massachusetts. Preparing and protecting yourself from bankruptcy by having a good policy to cover big emergencies aren't a bonus; they are a necessity for any small business owner.

Traditional policies offered to small business owners allow for more frequent trips to the doctor and the traditional low copay for office visits, but the premiums on those policies are extraordinarily high.

Whichever policy you choose, the premiums for your coverage (and in some cases those for your family as well) are tax-deductible expenses. Be sure to include them on your monthly expenses and to deduct the costs from your taxable income for IRS payment purposes. In addition, contributions to a qualified HSA are deductible.

In addition to health insurance, if your pet-sitting income is going to be a significant portion of your livelihood or the sole support for your family, you need to explore options for disability coverage. Policies include short-term, long-term, and even lifetime coverage. Pet sitters are faced with working alone and with varied animals, so a good disability policy can be a valuable insurance tool.

When you are looking for disability insurance:

- Determine your costs for maintaining your home and lifestyle (within reason). Calculate food, clothing, shelter, utilities, mortgage payments, car payments, etc., so that you can accurately assess your needs.
- Research well-known companies for policies.
- Make sure the policy you select provides coverage for self-employed individuals.
- Understand what the policy covers: waiting times, amounts received.

Saving for a Rainy Day

As a self-employed individual, you should set aside some money in a savings account each month. The money will not only help even out the slower months of January and February but will also help if a contracting economy comes your way or a major city-based corporation moves out of your area, taking with it most of your midday dog-walking clients.

Ideally you should save three to six months of your living expenses if you are the sole wage earner for you or your family or in combination with other wage earners if other people in the household are contributing to living expenses. This account should be viewed as an emergency fund. It is separate from your business savings account, which will hold money set aside for your tax liabilities. Your emergency fund will help you when the transmission goes out on your car and allows you the funds to dip into when times are slow.

Planning for the Future

As a self-employed business owner, you must plan for your future and your retirement. Fortunately some great options are available to you both in the tax-deductible and tax-deferred areas. As with other areas involving the law, the government, and money, these options frequently change. Be sure to do some research and make sure you know the current deduction amounts allowed, the tax-deductible or tax-deferred status of each, and your eligibility for each plan.

The first option is the SEP (simplified employee pension) plan. This is a tax-deductible retirement plan to which you can contribute up to 20–25 percent (depending on the legal structure of your business) of your earnings or up to $49,000 annually. The SEP is easy to set up and has low or no costs to administer. Another option is a Roth IRA. The money you invest is taxable income, but the investment grows tax deferred, which amounts to a huge tax savings over the long run. You can invest up to $5,000 annually for an individual and $10,000 for couples. In addition, if you are over the age of fifty, you can contribute an additional $1,000.

You can invest in both an SEP and a Roth IRA as a self-employed individual. You should invest 15–20 percent of your total take-home pay into one or both of these retirement vehicles to ensure that your future is comfortable long after you've retired from pet sitting. Most plans can be set up to take deductions from your bank account automatically, making your savings effortless. Deductions from your account can be minimal to start with and can increase as your profitability rises. In addition, the amount withdrawn from the account can usually be changed with most plans as needed.

There are some other investment opportunities through annuities and other products. To get a more detailed explanation or to set up an SEP or a Roth IRA, you should consult an individual investment broker, your bank, or your insurance company.

Other plans for self-employed individuals are:

- Keogh accounts
- Individual 401(k) plans
- Simple IRAs

Your complete business financial, insurance, and investment package includes:

- Business checking account
- Business savings account

- Emergency fund
- Health insurance coverage with possible health savings account (HSA)
- Disability insurance
- Retirement savings/investing through SEPs or IRAs (including Roth IRAs)

The Least You Need to Know

- Determining your hourly value and the costs of providing your service along with your market research will lead you to know the right price for your service.
- When you've determined your prices, publish a basic outline or structure on your website but avoid printing prices on hard copies that can become obsolete.
- Keeping track of your income and expenses on a regular basis is a responsible business practice and will make tax time easier.
- Be prepared to create a simple monthly profit and loss statement.
- Remember that you will have to purchase health and disability insurance policies on your own now that you are self-employed unless you have access to these via another job or a spouse's employment.
- Plan for the future by setting aside about 15 percent of your take-home pay for retirement through a Roth IRA, IRA, SEP, or other plan set up for self-employed individuals.
- Paying accurate taxes is your legal responsibility and should be done in accordance with IRS laws and your state's standards.

Action Steps

- Determine your price range for care through market research.
- Determine your costs for providing care (insurance, membership, etc.).
- Set up an income log sheet for client payments using a basic spreadsheet software.
- Set up a template for your monthly profit and loss statements using spreadsheet software.
- Research possibilities for health and disability insurance and determine approximate costs.
- Talk with your banker or insurance agent about setting up retirement accounts like a Roth IRA and an SEP account.

The American Marketing Association defines marketing as "the activity, set of institutions, and processes for creating, communicating, delivering, and exchanging offerings that have value for customers, clients, partners, and society at large." What does that mean in plain English? Perhaps a more easily understandable definition is one outlined in a 1993 article by Jan Welborn-Nichols, Market Arts, Ann Arbor, Michigan, a provider of marketing services for aspiring entrepreneurs and small business owners:

> ". . . marketing is everything you do to place your product or service in the hands of potential customers. It includes diverse disciplines like sales, public relations, pricing, packaging, and distribution."

Although we think of marketing and advertising as the same thing, and often you will see the terms used interchangeably even by industry experts, advertising your business is really only one piece of marketing. Marketing is everything you do to position your business in the market, find your clients, persuade them to use your pet-sitting business, and fulfill their pet-sitting needs.

The Four P's of Marketing

- Product (how will you differentiate your service from others?)
- Price (where will you set your prices in the range of market tolerance?)
- Place (what service area will you provide care to?)
- Promotion (how will you advertise your business?)

When we started our home-based pet-sitting business, we didn't go $5,000 or $10,000 in debt to get started. You don't have to, either. Start small, use grass-roots, face-to-face marketing, grow at a moderate pace, and you will be up and running within the year.

When you start your pet-sitting business, your focus will be on getting the word out to people that you are available for pet sitting in their area. To accomplish this you can spend thousands of dollars in high-profile advertising campaigns or hit the ground and put in some good face time and sweat equity to get more clients than a big impersonal campaign can buy you. Most big advertising is beyond the budget for most small businesses, especially home-based pet-sitting businesses. Billboards can cost $1,000 or more per month, radio between $500 and $3,500 per month, and television, even on low-cost area-specific cable networks, $500 a month. As you can see, these avenues aren't meant for a money-conscious home-based pet-sitting business.

A good marketing plan for a pet-sitting business will always keep in mind the perceptions of the target client. Perception is reality for consumers. How your pet-sitting business is perceived through your marketing and advertising will determine how successful you are in drawing in new clients. Make sure that both you and your materials present a good image of your business.

Identifying your target market will involve both geographical and customer segmentation. You will need to identify the customers who both reside in your service area and own pets that would require pet sitting.

After you've determined your target market, you will focus your marketing and advertising on influencing the people in your target market. Obviously it wouldn't do much good to distribute flyers or to advertise in a local apartment complex that isn't pet friendly. That's self-explanatory. By keeping in mind your target market and

When you meet someone, remember to present a good image of your business. Be friendly, energetic, enthusiastic, genuine, and interested in helping. The enthusiasm and energy you give off about your pet-sitting business will encourage people to use and recommend you. Make eye contact, be confident and positive.

the fact that all of your marketing should be geared toward
getting your message to the
people in that market, you can
also avoid being persuaded to
advertise in other venues that
don't sufficiently service that
market or that are too broad in
scope to include those outside
your target market. The latter
tends to be the case with the
larger media outlets like Yellow
Pages advertising, radio, and
newspapers. If your target mar-

The SBA suggests that you "learn to
know your customers better than anyone" and identify your target market by:

- Location
- Age
- Gender
- Education
- Income
- Interests

ket includes a certain type of pet owner in a geographic area, it is a waste of money
to advertise to people outside that geographic area. Find lower-cost ways to advertise and market your business to those people who will bring you the most reliable
sale. If, however, you will be providing care to the area that the Yellow Pages or other
large media outlets market to, it is a viable consideration. Just remember that the
more traditional sources of advertising are more expensive than grassroots endeav-
ors. You can always add sources like the Yellow Pages after you are up and running
and have some reliable income to pay for the monthly bill.

Now is the time to think outside the box and use your creativity in getting your
name out to the community.

Be sure that your advertising materials are neat, consistent, and contain a call
to action for clients (like a coupon for using your pet sitting or some other reason
to call you).

Keep in mind the needs of your clients. Make a list of what your target clients are
looking for in terms of fulfilling their needs:

- Convenience
- Reliability
- Knowledgeable care

Beware of advertising scams. About nine years ago we got a call to advertise for our local middle school band. The pitch was an 8-by-10-inch refrigerator calendar that was magnetic and would contain advertising from area businesses around the borders. There was exclusivity—no other pet-sitting or pet-boarding companies would be advertised, and the product would go out to the band families and be distributed at local band events. This sounded great. It was only $75 and included a double business card–size ad in full color. The profit made from the advertising would go directly to the middle school band kids who needed money for instruments. I mailed my ad copy and payment to the business address (a post office box—should have been a red flag) and waited for my sample product (most advertisers should offer you a sample or two of the product on which you advertised). Months went by and nothing came. I called the contact number for the company. It was no longer a working number. And my several letters to the post office box went unanswered and eventually were undeliverable.

To my dismay, I discovered that I'd been scammed. I did some research at the middle school, talked to the administrators and band director, all of whom told me that there never was a fund-raiser of that sort.

Buyer beware. Use only trusted sources for your advertising materials, and before you send money to a third party, do your research. This advertising scam comes in many forms: telephone book covers, wall calendars, refrigerator magnets, T-shirt printing. Reputable businesses provide services to groups seeking a fund-raising opportunity, so don't think that all of these requests are scams, but use caution. You should always request that your payment be written directly to the organization conducting the fund-raising and verify with the organization that the information you've received is legitimate.

This is also where you can set yourself apart from the other pet-sitting businesses in your market. Perhaps you can provide additional ways to fulfill client needs like:

- Last-minute bookings
- Specialized cat care
- Behavior consultation
- One-stop referrals to other professionals
- Grooming while pet sitting

You might take some time now to do a survey of potential target clients and what they look for (or would be looking for) in a pet-sitting business. You can do an online survey (usually free) at several sites online like www.surveymonkey.com and send it to friends, family, and other e-mail contacts. You can even link it to your Facebook or Twitter page so that more people can respond via mutual friends. If you're not comfortable with conducting an online survey, conduct a survey on paper. Use this information to tailor your business to fill those needs you see most frequently.

The better you can fulfill your clients' needs, the more successful you will be in filling your calendar. The better you are at conveying how you will fulfill the needs of your potential new clients, the more likely they will be to hire you instead of someone else. People are not buying just your dog-walking or cat-sitting service; they are buying the concept of a happier, healthier pet and a more convenient transaction for themselves. Draw on this idea of buying a concept to develop your business advertising literature.

Your advertising campaign should keep your message consistent through all media. Keep your colors and choice of words consistent and your logo prominent and visible.

You want people to recognize, at a glance, a shirt, flyer, refrigerator magnet, or car sign that is from your business. Think about some of the best advertisers in the world. Their logo, colors, and style are easily recognizable. They even go so far as using the same text font for their materials. Sometimes we can recognize the brand of an item before we are even aware of it. What works for the big guys can, and will, work for you.

Valuable marketing and advertising campaigns are tied to the number of impressions you make on a potential client. Impressions are the number of times someone comes into contact with your business. This can happen consciously, such as when a friend or veterinarian recommends your business, or sometimes these impressions are subconscious. People might see your car magnets or a flyer at a local pet shelter or pass by your booth at a pet event without consciously noting your information. If your materials are consistent, the client will start to tie these

Use caution with your logo because sometimes printers want to squish or stretch the image to fit into a particular template or size of product. This happened to my logo on baseball caps that I ordered from a startup printing business. Because my logo is vertically oriented, it was hard for her to fit the image on the low-profile baseball caps I chose. Instead of suggesting a different hat or asking about rearranging the logo or content, she squished the logo to fit in the space. The hats were still useable but would have had more impact if the logo's integrity had been maintained. Let printers know that you insist that the integrity of your logo or any other brand-specific items for your business be maintained.

impressions together. If your materials are inconsistent, it takes more work to make the connection. It has been said that it takes five impressions of a business before clients feel they can trust you and your business. Sometimes this is less in the case of a trusted word-of-mouth recommendation.

Have you ever received a flyer in the mail or seen an advertisement that appealed to you only to realize that nowhere on the advertisement did the business owner include the phone number, website, e-mail address, physical address, or any other means for you to contact him? These ads make it on the late night television shows sometimes in the comedians' review of weird and wacky headlines. It's a waste of time and money to advertise your business only to leave out the most important information—how to contact you.

The two most important pieces of your printed advertising message are the:

- Call to action
- Business contact information

Save money by having several people proofread any printed materials. Ask them to closely and carefully check for misspellings, transposed numbers in your phone number, and wrongly typed e-mail or website addresses. We wasted money ordering five hundred magnetic business cards only to discover that three of us had overlooked the fact that two numbers were transposed in our phone number. The cards couldn't be used, and we had to reorder all of them.

The Small Business Administration offers free online courses to get you going on your marketing plan. Log on to its website at www.sba.gov and click on "Free Online Training." Courses include:

Strategic Marketing: How to Win Customers in a Slowing Economy
Marketing 101: Guide to Winning Customers
Marketing for Small Business

The Great Car Graphics Debate

Advertising a pet-sitting business on a car is a highly debated issue among many pet sitters. Those who advocate magnetic signs, window lettering, or complete car wraps maintain that these are among the most advantageous and cost-effective ways to advertise. After all, you are in your car most of the day, and your message can be disseminated to thousands of people while you work. Opponents of car signage maintain that driving a car with your pet-sitting business information on it up to a client's home tells the world that the owners of the home are out of town.

Some options for having car graphics are:

- To buy magnetic signs that can be removed when you are actually on your pet-sitting runs
- To park around the corner from the house you are going to

Both of these options have drawbacks, though. If you frequently remove and replace your magnetic signs, they have a tendency to fly off the car when you are driving (not a good way to lose $60). If you have an emergency or are working in inclement weather (as might be frequent, depending on your location), parking away from your client's house isn't exactly a feasible plan. Perhaps the best plan is to have a car that has business advertising on it that you don't use for your pet-sitting visits and a car without advertising to drive to your clients' homes.

Weigh the pros and cons of this advertising method and do what you think is right for your business. Listen to the feedback from your clients if they are concerned about home security and do what's right for them and yourself.

The Key to Trade Show and Pet Fair Booth Success

Setting up a booth at a local pet event or even a big trade show can be a boon to your business if done right. We've all been to trade shows and walked down the aisles of vendors. There are the vendors who sit in their static, uninteresting booths waiting for people to come by, and there are vendors with whom you don't even want to make eye contact because they might be trying to sell something. Both of these are the wrong vendor approach to take when setting up a booth.

Draw people into your booth with something interesting to look at, compare, or, better yet, compete in. The easiest thing to do is offer a raffle drawing. People will enter the drawing by filling out a form asking for their name, e-mail address, phone number, and physical address. When you've completed the drawing and notified the winner, you still have a stack of potential pet lovers who might be interested in your business. Follow up after the trade show by adding those people to your e-mail newsletter list or sending them a postcard highlighting your pet-sitting visit and offering them a free visit if they book with the postcard.

An empty booth is suspect to passersby. Subconsciously we think that there must be something wrong with that booth or that it must not be that interesting if nobody is stopping to take a look. Enlist friends and family to mingle around your booth to give the appearance of activity.

You can also draw people into your booth by providing a demonstration. You can choose a pet first aid topic to demonstrate or the right way to fit a collar on a dog or even the various pet litters on the market these days and how to attend to a box with each. The topic isn't as important as the mere fact that there is activity in that booth. While the people are observing your demonstration, you can mention your contest or give-away and remind them to enter their name in the drawing.

Of course, booths can be a great way to communicate your pet-sitting business, what you do, and how you can meet the needs of the pet owner. Some people will ask questions and be interested in your service. They will likely pick up a business card and/or brochure. It is unlikely that you will book their care on the spot, so it is always important to capture the information of all people you talk to by having them enter your contest drawing as well. Then your job is to follow up with the potential new clients after the trade show or fair with an e-mail, phone call, postcard, or letter.

If you choose a nontraditional form of transportation, have a plan in place for a pet emergency. You might have to transport a pet to the veterinarian.

Even a paperless office needs a signed contract on file, so don't forgo that for now.

The Green Pet Sitter

If you are looking for a niche to fill and a way to set your pet-sitting business apart from others, consider being the eco-friendly pet sitter in your area.

To get started in a green way:

- Use public transportation, a fuel-efficient hybrid, fully electric vehicle, a bicycle, or a scooter to get to your clients' homes.
- Use biodegradable bags for scooping cat boxes or on your doggy walks. Or set up a Doggie Dooley (www.doggiedooley.com).
- Advocate for your clients to use eco-friendly products and be a resource for them to consult when they have questions. Suggest they use renewable and sustainable sources for their cat litter (Swheat Scoop, Yesterdays News, Corn Cob, Feline Pine), pet collars (hemp, cotton), toys, and ethically and humanely produced pet foods free of animal byproducts or drugs/hormones.
- Educate your clients on the hazards of the chemicals they use to control fleas and ticks both in their yard and on their pet. Suggest beneficial nematodes for the yard and herbal flea powders and tonics that are better for them, their pets, and the planet.
- Go paperless by e-mailing confirmations, taking electronic client notes, and leaving visit notes on a reusable dry/wet erase board or on 100 percent recycled paper. Take payments by credit card and let people know that your office runs on minimal paper by accepting e-statements from your vendors (cell phone providers, etc.) and your bank as often as possible.
- For each amount of a set profit that your business generates, donate money to plant a tree.

Don't Leave Your Current Clients Out of Marketing

The pet-sitting software we use allows us to run a report showing us the total dollars generated by each referral source we have listed in our system. The following list shows in ranked order our best referral sources for the years 2007–2010. By looking at this, you can see that our current client referrals are the best source of new business. I've left out the actual dollar amounts but we get seventeen times the dollar amount from client referrals as from business networking, three times the dollar amount from client referrals as from other pet sitters, and two times more from client referrals than from the next-closest category, the Yellow Pages. Why would you neglect working your best source for new clients? Focus on keeping your current clients happy, and they will send new clients to you.

Yellow Pages Directory		
Pet Sitter (Other Company)		
Vet		
Boarding Kennel/Doggy Day Care		

Your current clients are one of your most valuable resources for income and new clients. In pet sitting it is cheaper to keep a customer than to attract a new one. The small things you can do to keep your current clients happy will not only keep them coming back to you but will also likely benefit you twofold. As long as your clients are happy with your care, feel that you care about their pets and home, and are engaged in your business, they are likely to recommend you to friends and family. The better your care and service, the more talk your business will get from your clients.

A happy client will sell your business and care for you. Word-of-mouth referrals work so well because the potential new client has received the unsolicited and unbiased advice of a trusted person in her life, and that trusted person has already sold her on the benefits of using your pet-sitting business. That trusted person probably told her how great you are to talk to on the phone, how professional you were when you came over for the initial meeting, and how you left great notes for each and every visit you completed. That trusted person will tell her friend, family member, and coworker who is looking for a pet-sitting service all of the benefits of using your business and likely even give them an idea of the costs. When that new client calls you, the deal is pretty much done. She is ready to book.

Keeping your current clients happy means providing them with care that exceeds their expectations each and every trip. It means being consistent with your care so that they know what to expect each time they come home. They are relaxed in returning from a trip and know that you will have not only provided outstanding dog walking for their beloved baby but also have swept up the dog hair, washed out the bowls, watered the plants, and even run the vacuum. Consistency is key in the care you provide. Your clients will come to expect the level of care from you that you set. It is important to maintain this level consistently. The more that clients know that they can depend on things being done a certain way, the more relaxed they are in using your services and returning from a trip. There's not a single thing you can do that is more important to the success of your pet-sitting business than to provide quality care to your current clients.

Some added touches that keep your clients actively engaged in your business include:

- Thank you cards for becoming a new client
- Pet birthday cards
- Business anniversary cards (one year with your business, two years, etc.)
- Phone calls and e-mails just to say hello and check on the fur kids
- Thank you cards (and discounts) for referrals they send you

Use nationally marketed days like Take Your Dog to Work Day from Pet Sitters International or events like Wishbones for Pets (www.wishbonesforpets.org) to highlight your business' involvement in helping shelter pets. Invite your current clients to participate in celebrations, food drives, and fundraising events centered around these pet events.

- Frequent client discounts (similar to frequent flyer miles)
- E-mailed or snail-mailed newsletters with interesting pet topics and tips
- Special client appreciation parties at your home or local dog park

Your clients should feel as important, connected, and engaged with your business a year or more into your business relationship as they did when they first called you and you put forth the valiant effort to gain their business. Too often businesses expend so much energy attracting new clients that they leave their current customers feeling neglected or forgotten.

An easy and economical way to stay in touch with clients is to send them e-newsletters through services like Constant Contact or Mail Dog. The templates are fairly easy to use, and both systems price out plans for low-volume e-newsletters, making it an economical, timely, easy, and eco-friendly way to stay in touch with your clients.

E-mails and e-newsletters are great, but sometimes nothing beats the feel of a real paper card in your hand. Stock up on and take the time to write a thank you card for every person or business that sends you a referral.

Always, always, always ask and document where new clients got the information about your business. When they book their dates with you for the first time, ask them how they found out about you. If it was their veterinarian, their coworker, their groomer, their dentist, send a thank you card immediately. Include a coupon for pet sitting (or a gift card for a fast food or donut restaurant for folks like your veterinarian or groomer who don't use pet sitting). These personal thank you cards go a long way in showing your gratitude and continuing to receive those referrals. If you get consistent referrals from someone (like a groomer or another pet-sitting business), consider sending something more like a gift basket. An attitude of gratitude will show that you care about your business and theirs. Don't know the address of a referral? Look it up on the Internet or call the person and thank her in person and ask for her address.

Using the Internet to Market Your Business

Building Your Website

A well-built website is your best marketing tool. You can share reams of information about who you are, what you do, and why you are the best choice for pet sitting. The information can also be changed frequently if you have access to your site (which you should require from any designer or template you use). Getting all this information into a brochure or onto a business card isn't feasible. Changing your printed materials isn't easy or cheap. The fact that you can link your website with all of your information through pet-sitter listings and directories and national organizations is, well, priceless. People searching the Internet will likely run across one of these well-advertised sites more often than yours simply because of Internet listing frequency. People will type in their zip code and with a few

clicks be on your home page. You cannot give up this link to your clients.

Even if you aren't a tech-savvy person, make it a priority to get a website up and running. You can use easy-to-use templates or can get a friend to help you work through a template design. Most of the templates are point-and-click and designed to be user-friendly. In addition, some pet-sitting directory companies offer the service of building a website for you.

Make sure to maintain your branding in your website. Use your company colors and a good digital image of your logo. The look of your website should mimic the look of your other marketing and advertising materials.

Keep your website simple and easy to navigate. A basic website should include the following pages:

- Home page
- Services/Rates
- About Us
- Contact/Book a Date
- FAQ

Your home page should have small graphics and/or a photo. Be careful of large photos. They take too long to download and may delay your home page from opening. Include your logo in the upper left-hand corner of your page and prominently display your contact information (phone number and e-mail link at the least and a post office box for snail mail if you have one) toward the top of your home page. Links to the other pages in your website should appear along the top of the home page (and all other pages) and/or down the left side of the page.

Display all of the important information you want your visitors to see in the area that is visible without scrolling. This area is sometimes called "above the fold." That's a newspaper term referring to placement of the lead story above the fold of the newspaper. You don't want your visitors to have to search for the most important items on a page. Those items on your home page will be your logo and your contact information and some basic text on your services as well as the links to the other pages in your website. Be sure to include your contact information on your home page (and possibly even on every page of your website). It is frustrating to visit a website only to have to dig through pages to find out how to contact the business for more information or to book care.

Including a video on your home page is a sure-fire way to set your business apart and to move the client from interested to a booked visit.

Most important, your home page should be content rich. Include as much text as possible to accurately describe your services. Doing this will help maximize your exposure to web crawlers. "Web crawlers" sound like something you would want to avoid, but they are actually a web marketer's best friend. These automated crawlers seek out pages for search engines so that when someone types "Pet Sitting Biloxi" into the search box of his favorite search engine (Google, Dogpile, Yahoo!, Bing, etc.), appropriate pages are pulled up that the searcher can use. Although a picture can be worth a thousand words and will go a long way toward an emotional response from your website visitors, keep in mind that web crawlers do not use photos for content (unless you have content behind the photos). To maximize the results for search engines, be sure your home page has accurate text on the services you provide, your service area, and some key words like pet sitting, pet sitter, in-home pet care, etc.

Web crawlers work without any initiation on your part. They are initiated by the search engine. The world of search engines is a competitive market, and the better results a search engine can give to its user, the more often that user will come back. For this reason, search engines actively seek out new information on the web. This is

The worst mistake you can make on your home page is to have what's called a "door" or "window" where you have to click a picture or graphic to enter the site and there isn't any content or metatags. Home pages like these can sometimes be hard for search engines to find.

a great leap forward from the late 1990s when the only hope you had for attracting search engines was the metatags behind your pages. Metatags are still used today, and if you are having your website professionally built, your designer should include metatags. If you are using a template, look to see if there is a place to add metatags. These are the same key words you want to use in your content on your home page.

Services and Rates

Your "Services and Rates" page should set forth in an easy-to-understand format what services you provide (and possibly those you don't) and the general prices that go with those services. Your prices can be listed as a range of rates, and you can include a disclaimer that states that some pets and homes may require more time and care and that the listed prices are subject to modification after the initial interview or pre-service visit. Keeping your rates hidden to get the customer to call you for more details rarely works in converting the client who is fishing for information into a bookable client. Use your home page and "About Us" page to highlight the unique qualities, attributes, and services that your pet-sitting business offers, and clients will understand your pricing. If you've done your research, chances are that you are in line with the area competition and where you need to be to make a fair profit over your costs.

> The "Services and Rates" page is a good place to either list or link to your policies. It's important that your clients know up front what the business policies and practices are.

About Us

The "About Us" page should include a picture of you with a pet(s) if possible and any partners in the business. If you hire employees or independent contractors, you might consider including their pictures as well. Remember to keep your photographs small so the download time is fast. You don't want a potential new client to get frustrated and leave your website before finding out what sets you apart from all of the other choices in pet care.

The "About Us" page should tell the reader:

- Why you started your pet-sitting business

- How long you've been pet sitting (this can be tricky for new businesses, so you can include this at a later date if you are more comfortable with that approach)
- What qualifications you have
- What sets you apart from others in your industry

The "About Us" page should have a personal feel to it. Gear your writing toward putting your best foot forward and highlight the ways in which you and your pet-sitting business can meet the needs of your clients. This is also a good place to put a "Request Referrals" link so the client can e-mail you and request a list of people who've used your pet-sitting service and can vouch for your business. It's a good business practice to keep your referral list private and e-mail it only to potential new clients asking for it rather than publishing the names and phone numbers of clients on the web. In addition, you will want to have authorization from anyone appearing on your referral list. You can send an e-mail to a good client asking her if you can use her on your referral list. When she says that she would be happy to give an opinion of your business, print that e-mail and include it in her file.

Contact Us/Book a Date

It's a good idea to include your contact information on every page in your website. It might seem redundant to have a page that is exclusively for contact information if your phone number and e-mail links are elsewhere, but this is one item you want to make easy for your clients to find no matter what their web-browsing style is. There are standard ways that many web pages are set up, and people who browse the web come to look for those items on certain pages. Some people look for a separate contact page from the beginning, and others look for that information at the top or bottom of a page. Make it easy for your potential new clients to contact you. It can mean the difference between a new booking and a lost customer.

You can also include on your website a form or even just a separate e-mail link so that your current clients can go to your website and send an e-mail twenty-four/seven to request services. This is a nice convenience for both the client and you and has worked well for many pet-sitting businesses. If you use some of the pet-sitting software programs, a bonus is that you can embed a link directly to your booking system so that clients can access the system and book their dates. You simply go in and approve them, and your clients are all set for care.

FAQ (Frequently Asked Questions)

Most new pet-sitting clients have certain questions, and answering those questions on a FAQ page is a good idea:

- Are you always going to be my pet sitter (just one sitter or multiple sitters)?
- Do you work on holidays?
- How much do you charge?
- How long are the visits?
- Does my pet need to be current on vaccinations?
- Can you walk my dog during the visits?
- Can my neighbor do mornings and you do evenings?
- What does your care include? What exactly do you do?
- What happens if my return is delayed or something happens to me while I am gone?
- What are my payment options?
- Do you do your initial meetings only Monday through Friday?
- Do you provide boarding?
- What happens if my pet gets sick?
- What emergency plans do you have for weather?
- Do you have a backup in case something happens to you?
- Do you have any services like giving medications or playtime that you charge extra for?
- How long have you been in business?
- How do you handle my keys?

Additional and Optional Pages

If you have more room to expand your site past the basics, you can include additional pages:

- Photo gallery of staff and clients
- Links to animal-related websites, humane society, etc.
- Book a date (separate from "Contact" page)
- Pages that highlight other areas like pet first aid, training, etc.
- Blog page

Tips to Make Your Website Great

Keep It Simple

Keep important information and items "above the fold" (the visitor doesn't have to scroll down to see the information).

Don't overload the reader with text but do include content-rich text.

Keep pages short.

Keep links current.

Link your page to your page on Facebook, Twitter, and other social media sites.

Avoid Like the Plague

Confusing navigation

Misspellings and typos on your site

Broken or out-of-date links and information

Sound on your business site

Embedded tables

Intrusive advertising

Strange fonts or colors that won't show correctly in other browsers

Using E-Mail

E-mailing your clients to confirm the dates they've booked and to reiterate their pet care notes is always a good idea even if you aren't using a pet-sitting software program. Doing this puts something in writing, with a date, that you can fall back on should you need to research booked dates or changes in pet care. Get into the habit of confirming telephone conversations with a follow up e-mail and always tell your clients to expect to see something in writing when they book visits—either by e-mail or snail mail.

Blogging, YouTube, and Social Media

Stating the obvious here, the Internet is a quickly evolving medium. Be prepared to evolve with it. What is hot today may not be hot in a year or two. Innovations in web development, design, and promotion make the Internet a quickly changing venue.

Some of the newer innovations in the web are blogs, video publishing sites like You-Tube and Flickr, and social networking sites like MySpace and Facebook.

Blogging is a key component to your Internet presence. A blog will actually get you placed higher in organic (unpurchased web directory listing) searches because web crawlers will find key words in your blog and draw on those to link to your site when people are seeking pet-sitting services. In the last five years millions of blogs have been started. What's great about blogging is that you can discuss a topic like new eco-friendly pet products, and when people search for that phrase from their favorite search engine, your blog might come up, thus leading them to you and your pet-sitting business. This is good from a business standpoint for anyone in your area who needs pet sitting but also good all the way around because the more people who visit you and your website through your blog, the higher you will appear in local search rankings when someone is searching for a pet-sitting business in your area. It's all a very complicated algorithm that the search engine companies use, but suffice it to say that it is worth your time to blog.

Blogging is simply a news piece written by you (or someone else you hire or persuade to write for you) on any topic. It can be a diary of what's happening in your business, your opinion of the latest organic pet food, or a book review. A blog is just a written form of communication that is posted for others to read on the web. There isn't a set length. Blogs can be as short as a couple of sentences to as long as complete articles and reviews.

RSS (really simple syndication or rich site summary) feeds are the new way for people to read news and updates from frequently changing sites, including blogs. It's like getting a customized e-newspaper with only the topics and writers you are interested in. You decide what news is important to you, and you get it. Instead of your going to each blog that you enjoy reading or every news and entertainment site available, an RSS reader will send you updates when a new post is made to the sites you've subscribed to. In addition, your blog site should have RSS capability to allow people following you (potential clients) to subscribe and get updates on your latest postings so they don't have to remember to check back for new posts. You can link your blog to Facebook, MySpace, and Twitter. Most of the social media sites are set up as RSS readers, bringing you the latest news from your friends and the people you follow through the updated posts you get on your home page.

Be sure to remind clients to subscribe to your blog and use a RSS aggregator (called a "reader" or sometimes a "feeder") like ones you can find at:

- www.google.com/reader
- www.bloglines.com
- www.netnewswireapp.com
- www.newsgator.com
- www.my.yahoo.com

Why is RSS important to your home-based pet-sitting business? For two reasons:

1. You should get comfortable using RSS to glean information from various pet-related sites across the Internet so you don't have to spend your time searching for new items to share with your clients and stay in touch.

2. You should know how to tell your clients to use an RSS feeder to get new updates from your blog that they can passively receive. Staying in touch means staying connected to your clients and establishes a layer of trust and relationship.

Your website might come with a blog set up already. If not, you can easily start one at:

- www.blogger.com
- www.wordpress.com

When you set up a blog:

- Be consistent in postings—a large percentage of blogs are inactive after just a short time.
- Mention in your blog key words that have to do with pets, pet sitting, dog walking, and pet care.
- Include your business information and website in each blog and link to Facebook, Twitter, and all other online media sources.
- Stay on topic when you post.
- Spell-check and proofread your blog before publishing.

YouTube lets you produce video commercials for your pet-sitting business. You can produce a fairly well-done video with an inexpensive home video camera (like the Flip camera) and upload it free of charge to YouTube. Then you can post a link to that video on your website. These are exciting avenues of marketing and advertising your business that weren't prevalent enough five years ago to use consistently, let alone free. Now they are part of the home-based pet-sitting business owner's arsenal of free marketing. Video is a powerful tool in selling your pet-sitting business on the Internet. You can publish a video of you talking about your business and the services you provide and your credentials, or you can show some of the services like walking a dog, playing in the backyard or dog park, or scooping a cat box with your fabulous method. If a picture is worth a thousand words, video is worth a million. YouTube is easy to use and can be an invaluable resource to drive clients to visit your website and to book dates with you.

Sites like Facebook and Twitter were created for individuals to share ideas (and pictures) with one another, but in the past few years, they've become a hot spot for businesses to connect with their current clients and an even broader scope of their potential target market through their clients' online connections and friends. Remember the importance of impressions in your business. Social media outlets give you a free way to post items that will appear on other people's pages for their friends and connections to see. That's an invaluable tool for your home-based business. It's hard to determine which social media sites will continue to be around for years to come, which will evolve into something different, and which will be replaced completely by something more innovative and appealing to users. Whichever social media outlets are out there, they are a marketing tool definitely worth looking at.

Lynn Terry with Click Newz (www.clicknewz.com) says that ". . . used correctly the social media services can give you a platform for brand awareness, exposure, networking, and a huge boost in traffic & sales. As a small business, or an online business, social media campaigns give you an edge over larger competitors. Studies show that most companies are not yet adopting social media, leaving a sweet gap for the 'little guy' to do big business in that space." Social media give you an authenticity and a connection to your client base that you should use as a pet sitter. You can snap a quick picture with your cell phone while you are at a visit and immediately upload it with the pet's name to your Facebook page or your Facebook Fan Page. Then in your visit note at the home, let the client know that you took a cute picture of her baby and that it's on Facebook. Invite the client to join you there. It doesn't get much more intimate than that. You can bet that your client will share that cute picture of her baby with friends and family and talk about what a great pet sitter you are.

Use your social media sites to keep your clients informed with timely pet tips, local pet events, and things that are happening in your business. Your social media

Avoid the pitfalls of social media.

Don't start full force without first familiarizing yourself with the site and how it works.

Don't always self-promote.

If you wouldn't say it in front of your grandmother, don't post it.

If you wouldn't want your mother or the entire world to know about it, don't post it. Think TMI (too much information).

Keep pictures of pets discreet. You don't want some ne'er-do-well to figure out who is out of town at any given time. Pet's first names are sufficient.

Avoid highly charged political or religious posts.

If you hire staff, have a "social media policy" outlining acceptable postings and practices while individuals are employed or contracted by you.

pages should be written as a way to inform your clients, not sell them. It gets tiresome to receive a sales pitch every time you log on to a site, but it's fun to read something new about pets and better yet to see a picture of your own pet and be able to share that with a friend. As Lynn Terry says, "There's a reason it's called 'social media' and not 'self-promotional media.' Keep that in mind when you are considering what you will post to your social media properties. If all you post is self-promotional links and requests, you will eventually become a part of your readers 'noise' and ultimately be filtered out. They may not unfollow or delete you, but they will begin to scan over your posts and tweets without even realizing it." Social media establish another layer of the bond of trust between you and your clients. You can also offer coupons, special offers, and deals to your social media connections that other people don't get. You can even post events, take surveys, and have contests that are all linked to your social media sites.

Many people say they don't have time for social media, but as a home-based business owner, you don't have the time not to use this free resource for connecting with your clients. There isn't a manual on how to operate each social media website. The best thing you can do is establish the goals you want to accomplish with your business through social media and get your feet wet by wading in and testing the waters. Social media aren't about using just one resource. Try out Facebook, Twitter, YouTube, Flickr, and the myriad other sites available to you. More social media sites:

- LinkedIn
- Digg
- StumbleUpon
- Seesmic

After you've tried some or all of these sites and gotten relatively comfortable, link them all together so that one post links to all the others. Sometimes it takes some behind-the-scenes work in each of the site's settings pages, but all of the sites are getting better about easing the connectivity so that when you post to one, you post to all, and thus your message and your business do, too.

Best Pet-Sitter GrassRoots Marketing and Advertising Ideas

Build a simple, informative website and drive clients to that site with a strong call to action on your advertising materials.

- Get referrals from friends, family, and current clients by arming them with referral cards. Entice them to do the work for you by offering a free visit for every new client they refer. You can also offer a free visit to the new client. Simply print your regular business cards and on the back add "Referrals always welcome and appreciated. Refer a friend, and you each receive a free visit!"
- Take cookies/snacks and a magnetic calendar imprinted with your logo and information to veterinarians, groomers, animal shelters, travel agents, and Realtors in your area. Include your card and information on the package as well as extra cards for the office to hand out. When you deliver your items to these people, ask for some of their information so that you can refer them to your friends and clients.
- Attend (or start) a local networking group for pet professionals. Groups might be comprised of only pet sitters or a combination of other pet professionals like groomers, trainers, and veterinarians.
- Volunteer at your local shelter regularly.
- Write an article for your neighborhood newsletter or community newspaper on a newsworthy pet topic and include your business contact information.

- Use press releases and pictures submitted to your local newspapers and television stations highlighting your continuing education by attending a convention or other newsworthy activity you are involved in.
- Host a pet wellness and adoption day for your community, bringing together rescue groups, trainers, veterinarians, and other pet professionals. Let the media know about your day.
- Host a grand opening dog party at a local dog park (or get permission from your city to use a fenced-in baseball field if your area doesn't have a dog park). Celebrate other dates with dog parties. Invite current clients and offer them a free pet-sitting visit if they bring a human guest with a dog.
- Attend a trade show and split the booth (and costs) with other pet-care professionals like groomers or trainers or other pet sitters who provide care in a geographical area other than yours.
- Offer to speak at a local pet event. If you are trained in pet CPR, are an expert on eco-friendly pet care, or have another interesting topic to give a fifteen- to thirty-minute presentation on, get on stage.
- Set up a booth at a local pet event and have a give-away.
- Offer special discounts. These can be for groups of people like military, retired, or senior citizens. The discount could apply to a pet(s) adopted from a shelter or a dog with CGC (Canine Good Citizen) certification. Determine how these special groups fit into your target market. By giving a special discount, you establish an automatic trust and bond with members of that group of people. They feel special recognition from your business and are likely to call you.
- Wear your logo. Have T-shirts, jackets, scarves, hats, bandannas, and anything else you can think of to wear imprinted with your business logo and/or name (remember to stay consistent just as in your printed paper materials). You have to wear clothes, so why not advertise at the same time? Be prepared to tell people what you do.
- Send thank you cards.
- Use your business phone for the majority of your telecommunications. You will undoubtedly be out and about most of your day, so give your doctor, your child's teachers and coaches, your friends, and anybody else your business phone number. When you answer, even if you know who the caller is, answer with, "Thanks for calling ABC Pet Sitting. This is John." Even if your optometrist doesn't need pet sitting, he knows you are out there.

- Set up a Facebook page for your business. Link your Facebook page to a Twitter account for your business and register at LinkedIn. Start searching for friends and invite them to connect with you.
- Write a blog and post videos of yourself and your work on YouTube.
- Send magnetic calendars for the following year in a "Thank you for the referral" card to all the local veterinarians and groomers in October. (Nice pet-sitting cards can be found through Sharper at www.e-sharper.com or through It Takes Two at www.ittakestwo.com.)
- Encourage people whom you refer to other businesses like your favorite veterinarian, groomer, real estate agent, and hairdresser to tell them that they were referred by you. To get referrals you have to give referrals. Be sure those referrals know you sent clients their way.
- Consider vehicle graphics.

The Least You Need to Know

- Marketing is everything you do from advertising and sales to product pricing.
- The four p's of marketing are product, price, placement, promotion.
- Beware of advertising scams.
- To get the most from your advertising dollars, gear your advertising to your target market.
- Keep your marketing message and themes consistent.
- Green pet sitting and eco-friendly pet care are the new open market for pet sitters.
- Current clients are your biggest referral source.
- A website is a necessity for a professional pet-sitting business.
- The power of social media to promote your business cannot be overlooked.

Action Steps

- Network with an area pet professional to determine a good trade show or pet event where you can split a booth.
- Research options for eco-friendly pet sitting.
- Determine three ways you will market to your current clients.
- Build your website.
- Join a social media website and research starting a blog.

Let the Pet Sitting Begin

The Phone Rings—Now What?

When your first phone call comes in, you will want to be ready to provide professional answers in a confident manner. The best thing you can do is listen. Use a spiral notebook designated solely to taking all of your phone calls and message notes in. This works better than Post-it Notes, phone memo pads, and index cards because you have a working file of all of your phone calls. This allows you to go back and look at your notes. When a spiral notebook is full, put the starting and ending dates on it and file it away. You will have an ongoing library of your notes.

No matter what is going on at the time, answer your phone in a friendly, inviting manner. If you can't do that at the time, let the phone go to your voice mail. This is especially important when you are working from home. If the kids are due in the door any moment, are running through the house with their friends, or your spouse is yelling at the broken lawn mower, returning the call at a more opportune time is a better choice. People are accustomed to leaving messages, and most will.

Whenever you are on the phone, smile, even if you don't feel like smiling. Smiling makes you feel better. It's virtually impossible to stay mad, frustrated, or sad for too long when you smile. Even if you're having a really bad day, smile. Your clients will "hear" your smile through the phone, and it makes a difference.

[Ring, ring]
You: "Good morning. ABC Pet Sitting. This is [your name]."
Client: "Hi. My name is Mary. I got your phone number from my friend who says you take care of pets."

[Write down caller's name.]

You: "Hi, Mary. You bet. We provide professional pet sitting in your home."

Client: "Oh. Okay. Well, I've never really used a professional service before. What do you do?"

You: "We come to your home and take care of your pets and all of their needs right there where they are happiest. We take care of everything they might need; feeding, fresh water, playtime, light grooming, walks. We can also bring in the mail and newspapers and do the things around your home that need to be taken care of while you are away."

Client: "Oh. That sounds good. I didn't figure you would do all that. How many times do you come out each day?"

You: "Well, it depends on your pets' normal routine. Tell me a little bit about your pets."

Client: "I have . . ."

You: [This is where you actively listen and take notes as Mary tells you about all of her pets and their normal routine. Write down pet names, breeds, and important information. Does Mary mention multiple cat boxes or doggy doors or medications? Does she mention any other times when people like friends or family have cared for the pets and what they did for the pets?]

You: "Great. It sounds like your pets would do best with our . . ." [Complete your recommendation for number of visits and length of time at each visit.]

Excerpt from Cathy's Critter Care Policies

Our rule of thumb for visits:

All pets must be seen at least once every twenty-four hours. We don't provide every-other-day service for any homes other than those requiring only plant watering. Any home with a pet must be seen once a day. We can start on the day after the client departs and end the day before he or she returns.

Dogs that have doggy door access or that stay outside with adequate shelter and cats can be seen as seldom as one time daily.

Indoor dogs without doggy door access must be seen a minimum of two times per day, but we recommend three visits (especially for crated pets).

Client: "Okay. That sounds good. How much do you charge?"

You: [When you make your recommendation for the care that is needed, know your price. If it sounds like you might need to make adjustments at the preservice visit, let the client know that, too.]

Client: "Okay. Let me think it over, and I will get back to you."

You: "Sure. No problem. If you would like, I can e-mail you some references along with my bonding and insurance information."

Client: "Yes. Oh, that would be great. My e-mail address is . . ."

You: "Super. Got it. I will e-mail those to you right away, and feel free to let me know if you have any questions at all about the services or anything else. I would be happy to answer them."

You also might get the booking right then, in which case you would continue after you quote her the prices with the booking:

Client: "That sounds great. So, what do I do now to get my care set up?"

You: "What dates are you looking at traveling? [Take notes and listen.] When would you like to get together so I can meet your babies?"

Client: "Well, I work during the day. Do you do any meetings in the evening or on the weekends?"

You: "Sure. How about next Tuesday or Wednesday at about 7 p.m.?"

[Get Mary's address, phone number, e-mail address.]

You: "All right. I will see you next Wednesday [Include the date so you can ensure that you and Mary are both understanding what "next Wednesday" means.] Oh, and Mary, who did you say referred you to our service?"

[Write that with your notes in your spiral notebook!]

Write on your calendar the dates for Mary's preservice visit and her dates for care. If you are using a pet-sitting software, enter Mary's information and dates and send a confirmation to her with a link to the policies on your website. If you are not using a pet-sitting software program,

> We use the term *preservice* visit in Cathy's Critter Care. It can also be called an *interview*, *meet* and *greet*, or anything similar. It is the meeting that occurs before the start of care.

send an e-mail to Mary reconfirming your appointment date and time, the dates for her care, and the specifics of the services you discussed. In addition, you might want to include an attachment of your references and your policies.

Always err on the side of caution by calling the client with a question. If you've forgotten if the feeding is one cup twice per day or two cups once per day, call and ask.

I've found it is best to book a preservice visit ten days to two weeks prior to the start of care when possible. Some clients won't call until the last minute, and if you can fit them in, that's fine. Avoid having your meeting too far in advance. Pet-care routines, medications, and plans change as more time passes between your meeting and the care. It's also easier to remember details the client told you that you might not have written down and more likely that the pets will "remember" you. There is also a risk in booking a preservice visit too long after the phone call during which it was booked. People forget about meetings they've booked long ago, and they are likely to pursue other options. It's one of the hazards of the business. Sending reminders helps keep them in the loop and solidifies your arrangement.

Be sure to actively listen to what your potential clients tell you and try to envision their pet-care routine while listening so that you can make an accurate assessment of your ability to help them with their pet-sitting needs and the type of services that would best suit them.

On the day before any scheduled preservice visit with a client, it's a good idea to call her and make sure she hasn't forgotten your appointment.

Most clients want to know:

- What you do
- How much you charge
- If you can be relied upon
- What your plans are if a weather emergency occurs or something happens to you
- How much notice they need to give you
- How long you've been pet sitting
- If you can give medications
- If you charge extra for any services they might need
- If you can walk their dog

When we book a preservice visit we also send an e-mail like this one that helps clients better understand what we need from them (information and payment) and gives them a framework of how much time the meeting will take:

Thank you for choosing Cathy's Critter Care for your pet-sitting needs while you travel. We are looking forward to caring for your pets and your home. When we meet for the preservice visit on Wednesday, June 23, we will go over all of the important information that I need to take care of everything while you are gone. Some things you might want to have handy include:

Phone numbers where you can be reached while away

Your veterinarian's information (phone, address, and directions from your home)

A local emergency contact (friend or family member you would trust to make decisions should you be unavailable at anytime)

Some notes on your pets' routine, including feeding, exercise, and daily habits

Any information that might be helpful to us for their care

The meeting should take only about thirty minutes of your time. If you have any questions, please don't hesitate to ask me then or feel free to contact me here anytime (210) 945-8940. Since you are a new client, I will also be picking up payment for your services. We accept Visa, Discover, MasterCard, cash, or checks for your convenience. For a current copy of our policies and rates, visit our website at www.MyPetsitterOnline.com. Please let us know if you have any questions.

Thank you again for entrusting your home and pets to my care. I hope to provide you with worry-free travel and your pets with the quality, professional care they deserve.

Best regards,

Cathy Vaughan

At the preservice visit you will meet with the client and interact with her pets. This is one of the most important aspects of your job. You reflect what your company is. Speak clearly, be cordial, and appear professional yet warm. Make a good first impression with lasting memories. Wear one of your company logo shirts if you have them and other appropriate and professional attire to your meeting with the client. You should avoid wearing old clothes with holes, cut-offs, and miniskirts that are too short or shirts with anything printed on them other than your business because this clothing doesn't convey a professional appearance. You should refrain from smoking before and (obviously) during the meeting. This is probably your first chance to make a face-to-face impression on the client. This might be the one and only time you visit with her over the course of several years of caring for her pets and home. How you arrive will be how she remembers you. It is important to convey a professional, neat, and organized image. Avoid wearing baseball caps or visors to the first meeting. Some pets are afraid of them, and until you know, you want to make a good first impression with both the client and the pet. Some clients might offer you a drink while at the meeting. Unless it is absolutely necessary (water), refrain from accepting drinks, especially alcohol of any type.

A good starting place for the meeting is your presentation book, which will include:

- Business cards and brochures you can give to your client
- Your business license after registering with the county
- Membership information for any professional groups to which you belong
- Professional certifications from additional training (certification, pet first aid, and CPR)
- Thank you notes and referrals written by other clients
- Insurance and bond information
- Code of ethics or standards of practice for professional pet-sitting services
- Any press releases for your business
- Pictures of you with your clients' pets and your own pets and any other interesting pictures of you at community events and elsewhere—they speak a thousand words
- Handouts to give clients on topics such as heatstroke, hypothermia, bloat, dog-walking safety, good pet nutrition, and personal safety
- Service agreement, policies, references

You can skim through the materials in your presentation book but don't take too long. The focus of your visit should be getting to know the client and her pets. Take your service agreement/contract or similar document with you in your presentation book and fill it out in its entirety. Make sure that you and the client sign the form because this serves as a legal document for your visits with the client for these services and (if using the form on pages 174 and 175) for future services.

The preservice visit should take you between thirty and forty-five minutes to complete, but in the beginning it might take you a bit longer as you get more

Preservice Visit Checklist

Client service agreement/contract:

- ❏ Fill out and sign form
- ❏ Have client sign form

Be Sure You Write Down:

- ❏ Complete address, all phone numbers, e-mail address
- ❏ Dates and times leaving for and returning from their trip
- ❏ Dates for care
- ❏ Number of visits on specific dates needing care
- ❏ Pets' names and vital information
- ❏ Additional services requested (scooping yard, picking up mail, bringing in newspaper) checked off if needed
- ❏ Medication discussed
- ❏ Location of all feeding supplies (bowls and food)
- ❏ Feeding instructions discussed in detail. How much? How often?
- ❏ Location of all other pet supplies (leashes, brushes, toys, litter boxes)
- ❏ Location of mops/cleaners/vacuum
- ❏ Plant care
- ❏ Alarm codes and procedures, including a password should the alarm go off
- ❏ Veterinarian (name and contact information)
- ❏ Local emergency contacts
- ❏ How can the client be reached while away?
- ❏ Do any persons have authorized access to the house while the owner is away?

comfortable with talking to people. Before you leave the preservice visit, make sure that you have all the information you need to provide superior care for your client. Make sure you have a signed and completed service agreement/contract. If you require payment in advance from new clients, make sure you receive payment.

Many clients now have electronic surveillance of their home (i.e., a nanny cam). So always conduct yourself in a client's home like you are being filmed.

Get as much information as you can from your client. What color are the bowls, and what are the specific locations of items? Write your information so that in the future you won't have forgotten the details the client told you. You can refer to your notes and next time know exactly what to do.

At some point you might get a phone call from a new client wanting care but lacking time to meet with you before he leaves. We've had people call us with an hour or two of notice or on their way to the airport. Be wary of these calls. Not only do you not know what kind of pets and home you are walking into, but also there's a good chance that people who wait until the last minute might not be good paying clients. It's not a good situation all the way around.

Be careful not to promise what you can't provide. It's always a good idea to underpromise and overdeliver. It's easy to get swept up in the moment and promise to provide services that you can't fulfill because you want the client to be happy with the meeting. Be honest about what you can and cannot do.

When you return to your home office, prepare a file folder and put the client's contract in the folder along with any other papers she might have given you with prewritten instructions.

- Code the client's key securely.
- Write the date of the preservice visit on the file folder.
- Secure paperwork and key separately and safely.
- Let the pet sitting begin.

Now that you know what to do for a client, let's get to work. The items in this section are an overview of what we do in our pet-sitting business. You might want to add to them or take away some things that don't work for you. But these are the methods we've used and been successful with. We leave a visitation log (also called a "visit note," "report card," or "diary" in our industry) for the client with a note from every visit as well as a "thank you/welcome home" card and a small gift for the client or pet. The pet sitter should strive to do the extra things like scooping the yard, performing a quick vacuum of the home, or sweeping up consistently to ensure that the client comes home to a pleasant situation. If your client comes home to tumbleweeds of hair and litter tracked across the floor, her experience isn't going to be as positive as if she comes home to an attended-to house. Of course, your job is pet sitting, not housekeeping, but doing small chores makes the client's experience better. Clients appreciate the effort and are more likely to call you back again. Do your best to leave the home in better condition than when you arrived. The pets should be well cared for and the home attended to as well. A good way to make sure you are meeting the needs and exceeding the expectations of your clients is to leave a survey that they can mail in to you. Ask them what they liked best and what you could improve on. Take the comments to heart and use the feedback to make your pet sitting even better.

Over the course of your work, you will take care of many kinds of homes. People live in different ways. Some people keep immaculate homes, ask that you remove your shoes, and wipe down the sinks every time you are in the home. Other people are less concerned about housekeeping and might fall below your standards for a well-kept home. And many others will fall somewhere between the two extremes. It's important as a professional pet sitter to know your boundaries. You are there to care for the pets, and as long as they are being sufficiently attended to, then it is not generally in our realm of duties or legal obligation to concern ourselves with the living styles of other people. The longer you pet sit, the more you will see. Keep an open mind and understand that people are different, and that's okay. You ultimately decide for whom you will and won't work. If you feel strongly about the way a person lives, you always have the option of letting the client go to another business better suited to him or her.

Air fresheners are a good way to keep the home fresh, but beware of candles. Forgotten and unattended candles have been the culprit of many insurance claims. In addition, do not use air fresheners, candles, or wall fresheners around birds. They can be deadly to avians.

At each visit you should:

- Provide fresh water for all pets in clean bowls.
- Feed pets per client's instructions.
- Provide treats per client's instructions.
- Clean all bowls, bottles, or other food and water items thoroughly.
- Clean around pets' eating areas (placemats, floor, wall, etc.).
- Administer medication per client's instructions as needed.
- Visually inspect all pets for signs of illness, distress, or behavior out of the ordinary.
- Spend time visiting with pets and providing interaction and attention.
- Service cages, litter pans, and yard as designated by client.
- Patrol house for pet accidents.
- Patrol house for hazards or security issues.
- Bring in mail and newspapers and any flyers, leaflets, or other advertisements left on client's property.
- Properly dispose of all trash generated by pet-sitting services. Dispose of scooped poop, food cans, and any other odor-causing items in outdoor closed trash receptacles.
- Ensure that all doors are securely locked and all pets are in appropriate areas.
- Fill out the visitation log.

When clients arrive home they should find:

- Their pets and home locked, clean, and safe.
- A thank you card from the pet sitter.
- Instructions to call the office to notify pet sitter of their return.
- Appropriate welcome home gift for their pet (only one gift per service).
- Completed visitation log.

For midday clients who are in town:

- Take dogs out for a walk or fresh air in a fenced yard for majority of visit.
- Give fresh water to all pets and provide treats/snacks if client chooses.
- Clean all pet areas/bowls, etc., as needed.
- Leave a note for the client noting you saw the pets and the time you were there in the log book or on the visitation log as provided.

Overnight Pet Sitting

If you choose to provide overnight care services, some things can be different from standard pet-sitting visits. Keep in mind when you set up your times for overnight care that there might be conflicts with other regular visits if the times overlap. If you agree to stay at the client's home for the duration of time between your arrival and departure, you will need to set up your overnight arrival time late enough so that you can see your late evening clients before you go. Some pet sitters set up their overnight client policies so that they arrive earlier but then leave to attend to other visits and return to the overnight client's home. Either way works fine. You have to determine which method is best suited to your business.

Not all pet-sitting companies provide overnight care, so this is an area where you can set yourself apart from the competition. Overnight care should be priced at a premium service amount. Some houses are comfortable to stay at, and it almost feels like you are getting a minivacation. That's not always the case. You often won't sleep as well at your client's home as you would your own, and frequently the pets will wake you up to go outside during the night. Keep this in mind when pricing your overnight care. Don't be persuaded to reduce your overnight price. If you provide this service, you will earn every penny charged at most houses.

We've had clients tell us that they need overnight care but that the rates are too high for them. They want to know if we have someone who can stay less expensively. In their words, "someone that needs a place to stay for a few days." I politely tell them that I don't hire sitters who need a place to stay and that I send out only current employees for any job. All of our sitters have nice homes of their own and pets that they leave behind to stay overnight at a client's home. Thus, the price of overnight pet sitting reflects the quality care the pets receive from the overnight sitter. I seriously doubt that any clients would really want someone staying in their home who "needs a place to stay." Sometimes your clients just need to be educated on what your standard services cover (late-night and early-morning visits) and often see that overnight care isn't really necessary for them after all.

Overnight Arrangements and Policies

- Arrive at the agreed-upon time each evening.
- Discuss your obligation to stay at the home until the agreed-upon departure time the following morning.
- Sleep in the location agreed upon between you and your client. You should be prepared to attend to the pets should they need you during the night (i.e., to go out to potty). The owner should let you know which bed to sleep in. You might take your own bedding (a sheet and a pillow will usually be sufficient).
- If you and the client agree that you will use the bed with the client's linens, you should allow enough time on the last morning of your overnights to "strip" the bed of the sheets and pillowcases.
- Discuss appropriate sleeping arrangements for the pets as well.
- You should provide your own food and drinks for overnight stays. Clean up any messes made, and if the client's dishes and/or utensils are used, clean them and store them properly in their original location.
- Ask your client about using the shower/bath facilities at the home. You should bring your toiletries such as shampoo, deodorant, and hair products that you will need and refrain from using the client's items.

When you leave a client's home, pause for a moment and ensure that the doors are all locked. Stop and make a mental note of all the doors you used and make certain you remember locking them. If not, check. It's easier to check a locked door than deal with an unchecked and unlocked one. When you put garage doors down, sit in the driveway for just a moment to make sure they don't pop back open. One of your biggest responsibilities is the security of your client's home.

Checks and Balances to Avoid Missed Visits

- Tell your clients that they should always see a written confirmation of some sort—by e-mail or snail mail.
- Have your clients agree to call when they are leaving their house to ensure that care has started.
- Offer to call your clients during your first visit and tell them to expect the call.
- Have your clients call you when they've returned.

A Good Dog Walk Gone Bad

You are solely responsible for the safety and well-being of the pets in your care. This is a huge responsibility, and thus you will have to take more precautions with your clients' pets than you might with your own.

Make sure you see every pet in your care every day. Even if that means only shining a flashlight under the bed to see bright eyes looking back at you, make sure you can account for every pet. For those pets you can handle, a quick assessment of the pet, like Pet Tech's Snout to Tail Assessment (www.pettech.net), each day is a good way to make sure. And note on your visit log that all is going well with a pet. In addition to the overall health of the pet, check to make sure that collars are properly fitted.

When you go out for a walk, ensure that the collar and leash are in good condition and appropriate for the pet.

Educate yourself on the various collars available on the market:

- Buckle
- Snap
- Martingale
- Slip/choke chain
- Pinch
- Triple Crown
- Breakaway
- Head harness
- Body harness

As well as the types of leashes:

- Standard fabric and leather leashes in varying lengths
- Flexible leashes
- British leads
- Martingale leads

Some pet sitters prefer to use their own reliable equipment with dogs that they walk. You will inevitably come to know the tools you are most comfortable with and carry those with you in case you are faced with walking a 120-pound mastiff on a flexible lead.

Acclimate yourself to your whereabouts:

- Be aware of your surroundings when walking dogs.
- Avoid blind corners when possible.
- Take note of approaching people and pets.
- Avoid talking on your cell phone or listening to music when walking a dog.
- Always use caution when entering and exiting a home. Pets have been known to dart out the door suddenly. Make sure you close doors behind you when going in and out of a house. Cats will sneak out a door that is left ajar.

A good way to avoid playtime with other pets on walks is to say, "Oh, he would love to say hi, but he's been feeling a bit under the weather lately." Smile and say, "Maybe next time." No dog owner wants her pet to get sick from another dog or to bother a dog that might not be feeling well. It's a good way to defuse the situation without going into a full explanation of the legalities of why you can't let the dog interact with the person or her pet. Another option is to say, "She would love to visit, but we are working on some training right now, and she needs to focus." In addition, neither of these options discloses that the owner isn't home.

When you are taking care of a pet, do not allow the pet to make contact with other animals or people. You might pass the owner of a dog that your client's dog loves to play with when they are out on a walk. But there is no way for you to know for sure how your client's dog will react 100 percent of the time. If things go wrong, you will be held accountable for any damage done to the pets and people involved. It's best to err on the side of caution. A good dog walk can go very bad in a split second. An old, worn buckle collar snaps, and the dog that was just at your side ends up in the middle of the street. The flexible leash you were using snaps as the dog darts around the corner. A jogger passes you, and for no apparent reason the dog you've walked a hundred times before lunges out and bites the jogger. Two dogs that know each other end up in a tangled mess of a fight without warning, and they are both hurt. These are the kinds of nightmares that pet-sitter insurance companies hear about more frequently than they want and the kinds of situations that lead to settlements sometimes totaling thousands of dollars.

They Want You, but You Don't Want Them

There are people out there who, for one reason or another, you can't work for or don't want to. The easy ones to turn down are those clients who are out of your service area or have animals that you just aren't capable of caring for in a professional manner. Keep a list of your pet-sitting network colleagues to whom you can refer these folks. Be sure to ask these folks to let the other company or sitter know that you referred them.

It's the latter classification of potential clients, the ones you don't want to work for, that can be a challenge to turn away. In the beginning of your business, it's likely that you will be willing to take whomever, wherever, and whenever. That's how most pet sitters who've been doing this for several years were in the beginning, too, and that's okay. You do have to establish your client base, and the more clients you are doing a good job for, the more new clients you will get by their referrals. But don't think you have to take everyone.

There will be people about whom you get a gut feeling. You might think to yourself like I did, "This just doesn't feel right." The client might be short-tempered with you, talk over you during your phone conversation, try to back you into a corner and convince you to do something you aren't comfortable with, ask you to stay longer or discount your rates too much. There are circumstances in which people like this mean you no harm, but there are also times when you'll run into people who are accustomed to manipulating the people in their lives and the system as a whole. If your gut (instinct, intuition, inner voice, or anything else you want to call it) says

---

Red Flag

If a client tells you that she has used other pet-sitting businesses in the past and goes on to tell you everything that the other business did wrong, remember that there are always two sides to every story. Some of our most problematic clients have been those who've been through one pet-sitting business after the other. Things might start off great, and the client lets you know how happy she is with the care, but often the relationship goes south after some time. This type of client tends to be one who doesn't easily overlook a minor mistake or mishap and holds you responsible even for things beyond your control.

there's something wrong, listen to it. Most pet sitters are in tune with the underlying issues in many areas of their lives. If this is the case with you, listen to your instincts. It's okay to turn away clients. You might have to turn them away during the initial phone conversation, during the interview, or after you've worked for them once or on several occasions. Sometimes in the industry we call this "firing a client."

Confrontation is never easy, and neither is turning away money. The good news is that the situation, if handled effectively, will be nonconfrontational, and the money you would make from this one client won't be worth the hassles you have to deal with when you continue to work for him. Of course, there are some instances of a minor personality difference or communication style mismatch. Sometimes we totally misread clients and, when given the chance, they prove our initial reaction to be wrong. Try not to react too strongly or too quickly, but understand that if your inner voice is telling you something isn't right, you should listen to it more often than not. It is important to deal with these instances in a nonemotional, business-oriented, professional manner. Do your best to avoid an argument. You will always come out the loser.

If you get the feeling on the phone that this client isn't right for you, continue listening for a bit, but tell the client that unfortunately you won't be able to help her. Offer to refer her to another business. This is an ethical and responsible way to handle the situation. You are being honest and nonconfrontational.

You might wonder if you should refer such a person to one of your trusted contacts. The simple answer is yes. It is up to business owners to determine which clients are right for their business. It isn't something you should decide for them. When you refer the client to another pet sitter, you can send an e-mail or make a phone call to the referred pet sitter and let her know that you've sent someone her way and the reasons you turned the client away. Let her know that the client might be a better match for her. It is important that you take care to express your opinions in a courteous and nonoffensive, professional way.

It is never ethical to speak or write ill of clients in any context other than providing some background information to the other business to which you've referred them. You should never write badly about a client online, and even though you might feel the need to warn other businesses about this person, you should avoid using any version of publicly blacklisting a client. Doing so usually only reflects badly on yourself. What you discuss pet sitter to pet sitter over the phone, based on facts, is one thing, but a public disclosure of any client's name, personal information, and other details is not an ethical approach to dealing with bad clients. You wouldn't want your business to be publicly scorned for a mistake you've made. The same is true of your clients. Remember the Golden Rule. You can have an internal business list of those clients for which you will no longer work. In our business we call this the "DNB list" (do not book). But this list is never disclosed to other sitters. Should another pet sitter ask you if you've dealt with a client before, you can answer her questions, but be careful to stick to the facts of the situation and don't let your emotions get the best of you. Be honest and be respectful.

If you realize at the preservice visit that you've gotten into a situation that you're not comfortable with, you will have to let the client know then. Politely let the pet owners know that you feel they would be a better fit with another business you can refer them to. This is sometimes easier if you approach your meeting with the client as a way for you to get to know them and vice versa so you both can determine if your business is their best option for pet sitting.

If you need to fire a client you are already working for, you will need to finish the services contracted if it is safe to do so. Shortly after the client returns from their trip, let them know that you will need to refer them to another business and would be happy to return their key.

In any of the preceding instances, the client will likely ask you what your reason is for not being able to work for them. Is honesty the best policy? Not always. It depends. Sometimes being completely honest with a client leads to a confrontational situation.

But sometimes it's better to ease out of a situation than to be brutally honest. You might think your client needs to know how hard he is to work for, but usually telling him so only backfires. Take the high road, and it's better in the end.

If you run across someone who quibbles about your pricing or questions your policies, your background, or myriad other things, sometimes the easiest thing to do is to tell him (politely and courteously) that you might need to refer him to another

There are certainly instances when you can be honest and nobody's feelings get hurt:

You are too busy to continue with longer visits or ones outside your service area.

You truly believe that another sitter can take care of a client's pets more effectively than you.

You are narrowing your business.

pet-sitting business or boarding option that would be a better match for him. Ouch! Seems a little harsh, doesn't it? It did to me, too, at first. Make sure you really mean what you say and are willing to let this client go if he is a better match elsewhere. It's about being genuinely honest and understanding that consumers have the right to choose the business that best meets their needs. If that business is yours, great. If it's not, then you've done your duty in referring the client to a business that might. Something interesting sometimes happens when you offer to find clients a different option. They decide they want you!

This development could be a good thing if you still feel the ability to work for the clients. This closes the deal, so to speak. By taking back the opportunity to use your well-respected pet-sitting business for their beloved fur babies, you've made them want to use you even more. It could also be bad if you really do need to let them go, and they want to use your business even more now.

The Pareto Principle—the 80/20 Rule

In 1906 Italian economist V. Pareto created a mathematical formula to describe the unequal distribution of wealth in his country. His observations led him to conclude that 20 percent of the people owned 80 percent of the land and wealth in Italy. You might have heard about this principle in other areas of your life. Many others have observed similar instances in which the 80/20 rule applies, especially in business. In 1940 Dr. Joseph Juran recognized this natural tendency and labeled it the "vital few and trivial many." Dr. Juran's observation that 20 percent of something is responsible for 80 percent of the outcome became known as "Pareto's Principle" or the "80/20 Rule." As you build your client base, you may find that this principle applies to your business. About 20 percent of your clients account for 80 percent of your income, and conversely about 20 percent of your clients take up 80 percent of your time or cause 80 percent of your business headaches.

The key is to find out who your top 20 percent clients are, see to their needs, offer them special opportunities like open house parties or special incentive gifts, and ensure that they are happy with your pet-sitting business.

The Pets Are Safe. Are you?

You will make many early-morning visits and late-night trips out in the dark. The nature of pet sitting means that you will be working alone. Doing so safely is imperative.

- Make sure other people know where you are, with whom you are meeting, and when to expect you to be home.
- Know where you are going ahead of time. If your meeting is after dark, make a dry run during daylight.
- Have your keys out and ready when entering a home or your car.
- Be confident and strong.
- Be aware of your surroundings.
- Take your cell phone with you everywhere and make sure it's charged.
- Consider an application for your smart phone like Silent Bodyguard.
- Consider carrying a personal protection device like a stun gun, Taser, Mace or pepper spray, pocket alarm, or kubotan (a small stick about 5 inches long and usually attached to keys that can serve as a self-protection device when used properly). Be sure you know how to use the device, or else it does you no good.
- Take a personal safety course.
- Lock doors behind you.

There are as many "what ifs" for you as there are for the pets in your care. Your best weapon is your head. Be actively conscious of what's happening around you. This means staying off of your cell phone while you are working, walking, and driving. Criminals take advantage of the weak and unobservant. Being aware and confident goes a long way in keeping you safe. Anything can happen at anytime, so being prepared is key. Consider taking a personal safety course or training in using a personal safety device.

Emergency Preparedness—Hope for the Best, Plan for the Worst

Being prepared for an emergency is half the battle. Good emergency preparedness guidelines for pets can be found at www.ready.gov. Your clients are depending on you to care for their pets no matter what. It is a good business practice to have emergency plans in place for anything you can plan for.

It is important to find someone who can be your personal backup should you have to leave town suddenly to attend to a family emergency or should you become ill or injured. This person might be your spouse, a trusted friend to whom you've confided your business practices and who can step in at a moment's notice, or another pet sitter with whom you've developed a good relationship and who can pick up your clients on short notice. Carry that person's information with you on an emergency card in your wallet so he or she can be contacted by emergency personnel if you are incapacitated.

Write down your plans for the following:

- Weather emergencies (especially those that would prevent you from getting to a client's home)
- Local and national emergencies (think of the September 2001 terrorist attacks)
- Personal emergencies (death in your family)
- Personal illness or injury

To make sure you are prepared for an emergency, make some practice runs through your plans so you can work out the glitches before the adrenaline of a real emergency clouds your judgment.

The Least You Need to Know
- Always put your best foot forward on the phone.
- You are responsible for the pets in your care and anything that happens to them or for any actions they take while in your care.
- Be prepared and be safe while working alone early mornings and late nights.
- Emergency planning is part of a good pet-sitting business.
- It's okay to say no to some clients.
- The Pareto Principle applies to pet sitting.

Action Steps
- Practice your preservice visit with your friends.
- Take a self-defense course.
- Write an emergency plan for inclement weather, area emergency, or your injury or illness.
- Educate yourself on the different types of pet supplies and equipment on the market.

"Never get so busy making a living that you forget to make a life."

—*Anonymous*

You've done it. You built your pet-sitting business, and it is thriving. Congratulations. Now you just wish you could have a day off. You might be working in some capacity seven days a week, with little end in sight. You are staring burnout right in the face. The mornings get earlier, and the nights get later. The days get long. You feel like all you are doing is booking more clients and running out the door to see others. You hear the old Dunkin' Donuts commercial replaying in your head that it's "time to make the donuts." Should you start cutting back on clients or expand and hire people to help you? There's no right answer. Only *your* answer.

Where do you want to go from here? There are just as many businesses that choose to stay small as there are those that hire additional help. Big doesn't mean better, and it doesn't always mean more profit, either. As Peter Shankman says in his online blog, "Small rocks in the customer service world. Small equals love."

If you decide to stay where you are and forgo hiring, it would be a benefit to you to talk to the owner of another pet-sitting business with whom you've grown comfortable and who provides pet sitting in the same area as you. Work out a plan between the two of you to help each other when time off is needed. Doing this will allow you a fallback plan when you need to get out of town for a much-needed break. Work out a plan on how you will handle payments and how you will let your clients know about your arrangement. Make sure everyone is on the same page with expectations and clear on the money side of the arrangement.

After you reach this point, it's also important to realize that you need to refer your new client calls to other, trusted businesses. You can't keep taking more clients and expect to be less busy. You also might take this opportunity to shrink your service area or decrease your client base in another way, like specializing in one type of pet care.

Hiring

Hiring is always a much-discussed topic between pet sitters. You will likely talk about it at network lunches and certainly at any conferences you attend.

The main questions are:

- Should I hire employees or contract with independent contractors?
- How do I find good people?
- How do I pay them, and how much do I pay them?
- How can I make sure they are doing a good job like I would?
- How many people should I hire or contract?

Independent Contractors versus Employees

One of the hottest topics among pet-sitting business owners is whether to use independent contractors or employees. We've done both, and thus I feel confident in speaking to both sides of the issue.

Most pet-sitting business owners are terrified of sending someone out unsupervised to do a job for a client they've been seeing for years. What if the worker does a lousy job? What if the worker doesn't even show up? What if he gives the medication incorrectly or commits any of the many gaffes that can come up when caring for other people's pets and homes? For this reason I believe that most pet-sitting businesses do best using employees, not independent contractors. If your biggest fear is losing control of the quality work your business performs, then employees are the way to go. If you prefer to contract with existing pet-sitting businesses to work for your clients with the methods and procedures they've outlined in their business model, then independent contractors might be the way for you to go.

As noted in *Entrepreneur* online, the definition of an independent contractor as outlined by the IRS is, "A person hired to do work for another but who is not an employee or agent of that person. Control is subjected to the end result and not as to how the work is performed as opposed to an employee who receives direction on what, when and, to some degree, how to do a job."

Here is a good example of an independent contractor being used in a pet-sitting business: You have a friend and professional colleague who is a certified dog trainer. One of your clients asks if you know of any good dog trainers. Actually you do. She is on staff with you. Instead of recommending her training outside your business, you hire this person inside your business as an independent contractor. You've set up with the trainer how much she expects you to pay her for training services for your clients. You quote your client whatever price you wish. Your client pays you. The trainer goes out at a time agreed upon, works with the pet, and invoices you for the services. You have no say in how the training is done, what needs to be done at the session, or how the trainer handles herself with your pet-sitting client.

According to the IRS, three areas are examined when determining the classification of a person working for another. What is the extent of:

- Behavioral control?
- Financial control?
- Behavioral relationship?

If you provide the people who work for you with specific instructions for conducting the work at a client's home or training on how to pet sit, you are likely to be viewed by IRS standards as having employees.

One thing is clearly stated by the IRS. Whether or not you call someone an independent contractor or an employee doesn't matter. How the person is used in his position and the manner in which he is instructed, controlled, and supervised does matter. Just because you call someone an independent contractor doesn't make him one.

The major drawback to hiring employees is in dealing with pay and benefits. As an employer, you will be responsible for half of the Social Security and Medicare payments made on their wages. However, these are tax-deductible expenses, so they do not come out of your bottom line. Most pet-sitting businesses that hire employees pay them less than what other businesses that use independent contractors pay. This is to make up for the difference in the tax payments made. If done correctly, it all comes out in the wash.

Another example of using an established pet-sitting business as an independent contractor would be when you decide that you need additional help during an especially busy time. The clients pay you their normal fee. You hire ABC Pet Sitting to care for three of your clients. You let your clients know that you are hiring extra help during your busy time and that they will be contacted by ABC Pet Sitting to set up a meeting. ABC Pet Sitting meets with the clients, performs the jobs with the appropriate number of visits to the clients' homes. The clients return and are happy with the care. ABC Pet Sitting invoices you for its contract work for the total amount of services performed. At no time did you provide instruction to ABC Pet Sitting on how to care for the clients it was seeing, nor did you supervise ABC's work.

In addition to federal taxes, employers in some states are responsible for unemployment insurance, worker's compensation payments, and other expenses as outlined by their state. This is the major reason why many pet-sitting businesses choose to use only independent contractors.

Now is the time when you need to hire a good CPA to help you decide the best route for your business. Making the wrong decision can cost you thousands of dollars if you are audited by the IRS. According to Entrepreneur.com, "If the IRS finds you've misclassified an employee as an independent contractor, you'll pay a percentage of income taxes that should have been withheld on the employee's wages and be liable for your share of the FICA and unemployment taxes, plus penalties and interest. Even worse, if the IRS determines your misclassification was 'willful,' you could owe the IRS the full amount of income tax that should have been withheld (with an adjustment if the employee has paid or pays part of the tax), the full amount of both the employer's and employee's share of FICA taxes (possibly with an offset if the employee paid self-employment taxes), plus interest and penalties."

Where Are the Good Pet Sitters?

When you decide that it's time to hire, your best people can be found from many sources. Some sources that have been successful for us:

- Clients
- Friends and acquaintances

- Previous coworkers
- Veterinarian
- Craigslist

Have a standard application that the potential new sitter fills out and conduct a background check on any individual who will be entering your client's home as either your employee or independent contractor. Conduct an interview and make sure you are honest with the applicant about the job requirements. Tell her the good, the bad, and the ugly. Otherwise you will hire or contract someone only to have her leave after a short time.

When you become an employer, be prepared to deal with the people issues that come with that responsibility. Your employees and independent contractors have lives of their own to lead and aren't as emotionally invested in your business as you are. They might seem as committed as you, but understand that your pet-sitting business isn't as much a part of their identity as it is yours. Behavior that seems to indicate that your staff members don't care really doesn't. Dealing with the full picture of staff issues is well beyond the scope of this book, but as you see your business grow and anticipate hiring people, start reading. How you communicate and deal with your staff will determine your continued success in pet sitting. Your staff will become a reflection of you and your pet-sitting business, and you want that reflection to be a happy one.

Payday

Most pet-sitting companies pay their staff by the completed visit. Very few businesses include drive time or reimbursement for gas expenses incurred by the sitter. However, some states require that a minimum wage be established, and the pay cannot drop below that point when figured on an hourly basis. If you decide that you will not reimburse for gas expenses, your employee or independent contractor can keep a mileage log and file for reimbursement of expenses on his or her tax return.

When you hire people, remember that you are in the business to make money. What you pay your staff should be less than what you charge clients and should allow you enough wiggle room to pull out your business expenses and still make a profit. Most pet-sitting businesses pay their staff in the range of 45–60 percent of the pet-sitting charge. Keep in mind that independent contractors may make more than this percentage and will certainly fall on the higher end of the scale. Allow yourself enough room to give raises as merited and reward your good staff members monetarily with bonuses.

Although most businesses pay in a percentage range, it is a good idea to have a fixed amount that you pay per visit. If you pay by percentage, then every time you increase your rates, your staff will also receive an automatic raise. This might not be the best plan for stimulating good work in your employees. Also, it minimizes the effect you can have in raising rates to cover higher business costs like rate increases from your insurance provider, your phone or Internet service provider, and other vendors.

A good payment schedule for employees is twice per month for all satisfactorily completed assignments during that time frame. As you grow and hire more people, you will need several days to process payroll. We pay for work completed from the first of the month to the fifteenth of the month on the twenty-third of that month. We pay for work completed from the sixteenth of the month through the last day of the month on the eighth of the following month. This arrangement allows enough time to make sure that all checks that have been picked up by the sitters are turned into the office and gives us a few days to verify payroll numbers. We use an online payroll system that submits the employees' pay direct deposit, making it convenient. In addition, the payroll system withholds the appropriate taxes and submits the necessary forms for us to the state and federal tax entities.

If you are paying independent contractors, they should submit an invoice to you to receive payments. Be sure to outline in your contract what the standard and acceptable time frames are for submitting these to you.

How Many People Do You Need?

If your schedule is full, and you are looking for time off, a good rule of thumb is to hire one person to take about three to five visits from your schedule about four days a week. Keep in mind this is a rule of thumb. You might find a great candidate for a staff pet sitter who can take a full day of eight visits two days a week. If she is the right fit for your business, then hire her. It's scary at first to see your workload dwindle from your schedule to someone else's, but remember that if you've set your prices and wages right, you are making some money off of every visit she does. Her schedule will be set (and likely filling up), and yours will continue to fill up again as you are able to accept more clients.

At that point it is time to hire someone again and lighten your load and possibly some of the load from the first staff sitter you hired. Neither you nor your staff members should be working so much that you feel like you have no life. If that is the case, it's time to hire or contract someone else. Before you know it, you might employ or contract with twenty-five different staff pet sitters and be able to still pet sit some, too, but also run the office. If running the office isn't what you envisioned for yourself, don't discount the ability to hire a part-time or full-time office assistant so you can get back to doing what you love: being greeted at the door by wagging tails.

The Least You Need to Know

- Your pet-sitting business will grow to the point that you will have to decide to stay small or hire help.
- Pet-sitting businesses use employees and independent contractors.
- Employees provide the employer with more control over the work.
- Independent contractors are easier to pay because of less-stringent rules on taxes and other benefits.
- Clients and your circle of acquaintances can be a valuable source for staff.
- Stay profitable when you hire staff members by analyzing how much you can pay them.

Action Steps

- Decide what your business goals are: to stay small or to grow.
- Consult with a CPA to determine which type of staff is best for your business.
- Hire additional staff members after a complete interview and background check.
- Set up with a payroll service to pay your staff members.

[Your Pet Sitting Business]

Client Information/Service Agreement

Name_____   Date_____

Mailing Address_____   Pager Number_____

City_____   Cell Phone Number_____

State_____Zip_____   Cell Phone Number_____

Home Phone Number_____   Office Phone Number_____

Home email address_____   Office email address_____

Date Leaving_____ Time_____   Date Returning_____ Time_____

First visit on _____ at _____am/pm   Last visit on_____ at_____am/pm

Total # of visits/nights _____ (x) $_____per visit/night (+) additional fees if any_____ =

Total Price $_____

Special Instructions for Visits/Time Requests_____

_____

Services Requested____Mail____Paper_____Alter lighting____Alter draperies_____Plant Care

_____Medicate Pet(s)____Scoop Poop in Yard _____Take out garbage cans.

Trash picked up on S M T W T F S

You can be reached at_____

_____

Pets			
Name	DOB	Description (breed,color,etc)	Temperament/Special Conditions/Medication
1)_____Medication_____			
2)_____Medication_____			
3)_____Medication_____			
4)_____Medication_____			
5)_____Medication_____			

Medication required and details_____

_____

_____**Location of Food and other Supplies**_____

_____

_____

_____**Location of Feeding Areas (Bowls)**_____

_____

_____

_____**Location of Cleaners/Mop/Brooms**

and Vacuum _____

Name_____   Phone Number_____

_____Additional instructions for care/feeding _____

_____

_____

_____Special Instructions and Notes on Pets_____

_____

_____

_____

Plant Care / Misc Info_____

Home Security Details_____

Local Emergency Contact Name_____   Phone Number_____

Your Veterinarian Name_____   Phone Number_____

Persons with access to your home while you're away (any visitors or anyone with a key to your home)

I have read and understand the services that will be performed by Cathy's Critter Care for the dates from_____ through_____. The pet sitter is authorized to perform care and services as outlined in this contract and to seek emergency veterinary care or home care as deemed necessary solely through the pet sitter's discretion. The pet sitter may adjust care from this contract for the safety and well being of pets and property if the pet sitter deems necessary. If client's veterinarian or other professional specified in this agreement cannot be reached or is unavailable, client authorizes pet sitter/Cathy's Critter Care to choose a qualified professional to handle the emergency. Client agrees to reimburse pet sitter/Cathy's Critter Care for expenses incurred, plus any additional fees for attending to this need or any expenses incurred for any other home/food/supplies needed. Pet sitter is entrusted to use their best judgment in caring for pets and home. Pet sitter/Cathy's Critter Care will be held harmless for consequences related to such decisions. Pet sitter agrees to provide the services stated in this contract in a reliable, caring and trustworthy manner. In consideration of these services and as an express condition therof, the client expressly waives and relinquishes any and all claims against pet sitter/Cathy's Critter Care except those arising from legal negligence or willful misconduct on the part of the pet sitter. Client understands this contract also serves as an invoice and takes full responsibility for PROMPT payment, as outlined in POLICIES, of outstanding fees upon completion of services contracted. In the event of personal emergency or illness of pet sitter, client authorizes Cathy's Critter Care to arrange for another qualified person to fulfill responsibilities as set forth in this contract. Client has stated that pets are not aggressive and have not previously bitten anyone.___Should pet sitter be bitten or otherwise exposed to any disease or ailment received from client's animals, it will be the client's responsibility to pay all costs and damages incurred by the victim. Cathy's Critter Care reserves the right to terminate this contract at any time before or during its term if pet sitter/Cathy's Critter Care, in its sole discretion, determines that client's pet poses a danger to the health or safety of pet sitter or others. Client authorizes pet to be placed in a boarding kennel if deemed necessary for any reason by the pet sitter/Cathy's Critter Care with all charges therefrom to be charged to client. Client authorizes this signed contract to be valid approval for future services of any purpose provided by this contract, permitting Cathy's Critter Care to accept telephone or internet reservations for services and enter premises without additional signed contract or writer authorization. Client agrees to abide by POLICIES for departure and return phone calls to Cathy's Critter Care office for future reservations. Cathy's Critter Care is authorized to keep two copies of house keys on file for future services unless expressly requested for return._____(keep/return) All future reservations must be made through the Cathy's Critter Care main office or this contract is void. Client has read and received a copy of the POLICIES for Cathy's Critter Care, and agrees to all terms stated within the policies. The client_____ or any person acting on the client's behalf waives any claims against any agents/employees/contractors of Cathy's Critter Care or Catherine Fereday-Vaughan or Phillip Wayne Vaughan for any loss, theft, or damage to property or pets not due to willful negligence. Any and all changes made to this contract must be sent to the Cathy's Critter Care office in writing.

_____   _____

_____[YOUR PET SITTING BUSINESS NAME, DATE]   Client signature   date

Additional Information and Detailed Instructions may be attached on an additional page.

ADDITIONAL NOTES:

Appendix A:
Additional Web Resources

www.business-insurers.com, Pet Sitters Insurance

www.entrepreneur.com, *Entrepreneur Online Magazine*

www.intuit.com, Website Design, Accounting, Payroll

www.IRS.gov, Internal Revenue Service

www.mourerfoster.com, Pet Sitters Insurance

www.nase.org, National Association for the Self-Employed

www.petraxsoftware.com, Pet Sitter Business Software

www.petsit.com, Pet Sitters International

www.petsitllc.com, Pet Sitters Insurance

www.petsitters.org, National Association of Professional Pet Sitters

www.petsitusa.com, Pet Sitter Directory and Resources

www.powerpetsitter.com, Power Pet Sitter Web-Based Software

www.professionalpetsitter.com, Bluewave Professional Pet Sitter Software

www.sba.gov, Small Business Administration

Index

About the Author

Cathy Vaughan began pet sitting professionally in 1998 through the encouragement of her husband, Phillip. She had left her career as a Zookeeper and Sea Lion Trainer at the San Antonio Zoo earlier that year to raise their first child. However, she quickly realized that making ends meet on one income for the family was a daunting challenge and she missed using her skills and passion for animals of all species. Cathy's Critter Care was "born" as a way to help the family budget and quell the daily desire to work with animals. Since 1998, Cathy's Critter Care has grown from a one client, startup business with Cathy Vaughan being the only provider of care to a business that employs 16 part time pet sitters and a full time office manager. In 2006, Cathy's Critter Care was doing well enough for Phillip to leave his full time job and begin working in the pet sitting business.

Throughout her 12 years as business owner, Cathy has served as a Goodwill Ambassador for Pet Sitters International, spoken at conventions and written articles that have appeared in the World of Professional Pet Sitting. Cathy has appeared on local television and spoken at local events to educate people on the benefits of hiring a professional pet sitter and the importance of responsible pet ownership. She is currently a certified Pet First Aid and CPR instructor through PetTech and continues to educate pet sitters and pet owners about handling emergency first aid situations.

Currently Cathy is focusing her efforts to expand Cathy's Critter Care. In 2010, she and Phillip, along with their business partner, Cynthia Gibson, will open the Bluebonnet Bunk'n Biscuit. This pet care facility will incorporate boarding, doggy daycare, grooming and a membership dog park and indoor 9000 square foot play area.